Contents

1	**Introducing Fireworks**	**7**
	About Fireworks	8
	Obtaining Fireworks	9
	Installing Fireworks	10
	The first view	11
	Menu bar and toolbars	12
	Tools panel	13
	Panels	15
	Properties Inspector	17
	Creating files	18
	Opening files	19
	Importing files	20
	Saving files	22
	Getting help	24
2	**Working with objects and images**	**25**
	Bitmaps	26
	Vectors	27
	Identifying selected items	28
	Points and paths	29
	Working with paths	30
	Resizing images	31
	Image editing	32
	Image retouching	33
3	**Creating objects**	**35**
	Drawing modifiers	36
	Drawing tools	37
	Adding text	40
	Viewing objects	41
	Adding fills	42
	Adding strokes	44
	Adding effects	45

Styles panel 47
Color Mixer panel 48

4 Editing objects 49

Reshaping 50
Orientation 52
Scaling 54
Skewing 55
Distorting 56
Arranging and aligning 57
Selecting parts of objects 58
Cropping 61
Cloning 62
Erasing 63
Selecting colours 64

5 Optimising images 65

Why optimise images? 66
Previewing images 67
Optimize panel 68
Applying optimisation 69
Export Preview 70
Export Wizard 71
Quick Export 73
Transparency 75

6 Web authoring with Fireworks 77

Fireworks and Dreamweaver 78
Roundtrip image editing 79
Resizing images 81
Creating Web pages in Fireworks 83

7 Slices, hotspots and layers 85

About slices 86
Creating slices 87
Slice options 89

FIREWORKS MX

in easy steps

NICK VANDOME

In easy steps is an imprint of Computer Step
Southfield Road . Southam
Warwickshire CV47 0FB . England

http://www.ineasysteps.com

Notice of Liability

Every effort has been made to ensure that this book contains
accurate and current information. However, Computer Step and the
author shall not be liable for any loss or damage suffered by readers
as a result of any information contained herein.

Trademarks

Fireworks® is a registered trademark of Macromedia, Inc. All other
trademarks are acknowledged as belonging to their respective
companies.

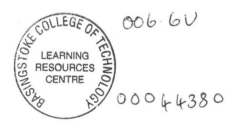
Printed and bound in the United Kingdom

ISBN 1-84078-234-X

Optimising slices 90
Text slices 91
Reconstituting tables 92
Creating hotspots 95
Exporting slices and hotspots 96
Creating layers 97
Web layer 98
Working with layers 99
Blending 102
Creating masks 103
Editing masks 104

Buttons and navigation bars **105**

8

About buttons 106
Creating buttons 107
Buttons and the Library 111
Editing buttons 113
Exporting buttons 114
Navigation bars 115

Rollovers **117**

9

About rollovers 118
Creating rollovers with behaviors 119
Drag-and-drop rollovers 122
Creating disjoint rollovers 124
Creating pop-up menus 127
Editing pop-up menus 134
Combining slices and hotspots 135
Editing behaviors 138
Exporting rollovers 140

Animation **141**

10

Animation in Fireworks 142
Animation basics 143
Creating symbols 144
Animation and the Library 146

Creating a simple animation 148
Animation settings 150
Optimising 153
Exporting 154
Editing animations 156
Onion skinning 157
Tweening 158

Extending Fireworks 161

11

About extensions 162
Applying extensions 163
Managing extensions 166
Obtaining extensions 167
Installing extensions 170
Using scripts 171

Automating tasks 173

12

About automated tasks 174
Find and Replace 175
Batch processing 179
Backing up batch files 185
History panel 186

Index 187

Introducing Fireworks

Fireworks is a powerful image editing and graphics design program, that is aimed primarily at Web designers. It can be used to create and edit simple images and graphics, such as buttons for Web pages, or it can handle more complex tasks such as creating rollover images and pop-up menus. This chapter shows how to obtain and install Fireworks and goes through the basic functions so that you can get up and running with the program.

Covers

About Fireworks | 8

Obtaining Fireworks | 9

Installing Fireworks | 10

The first view | 11

Menu bar and toolbars | 12

Tools panel | 13

Panels | 15

Properties Inspector | 17

Creating files | 18

Opening files | 19

Importing files | 20

Saving files | 22

Getting help | 24

Chapter One

About Fireworks

On the surface, Macromedia's Fireworks is an image editing package, of a similar nature to a program such as Adobe Photoshop. However, there are some very important differences. Firstly, Fireworks is designed specifically to work with images that are going to be used on the Web. It is closely integrated with the Macromedia Web authoring tool, Dreamweaver, and its main purpose is to give Web designers the means to create images for the Web and also manipulate existing images so that they are in the optimum condition for use on the Web. This involves creating file sizes that are as small as possible, while still retaining sufficient image quality. This means that the images will download as quickly as possible when viewed on the Web.

The term 'Web designer' can be applied to anyone who produces Web pages. You do not have to be a highly qualified professional. With programs such as Fireworks and Dreamweaver, you will be perfectly capable of producing websites that are comparable with those of the professionals.

But Fireworks is not just an image manipulation tool. Web designers can also create interactive features for Web pages using HTML and Javascript functions. All the designer has to do is create the elements that they want and Fireworks creates all of the code for them in the background. It is then just a case of exporting the end product into Dreamweaver, a task that Fireworks handles with ease. Some of the elements that can be created within Fireworks include:

Slicing is a technique in Fireworks whereby an image is broken down into smaller parts and then reconstructed when it is viewed in an HTML Web page. This means that different areas of an image can be edited independently of each other. For more information on slicing, see Chapter Seven.

- Add hyperlinks to images

- Create navigation bars

- Create pop-up menus

- Create simple and advanced rollover images

- Create hotspots and slices

With Fireworks it is possible to perform simple image editing tasks or create complex graphics, primarily for use on the Web. It is even possible to author an entire website using Fireworks, although it is more common to use it in conjunction with Dreamweaver. Overall, Fireworks is an extremely powerful tool that can make a dramatic difference to the production of Web pages. With its inclusion in the new Macromedia suite of MX programs (including Flash, Dreamweaver and Freehand) it has become part of a very versatile family of programs for Web designers.

Obtaining Fireworks

Fireworks is produced by Macromedia, the market leader in Web authoring software. Fireworks is their main graphic design tool for the Web and this is complemented with Dreamweaver for overall Web design and management, Flash for Web animation and Freehand for illustration creation.

Fireworks can be purchased from general software retailers, either in person or over the Web. It costs approximately £240–£270, depending on where you buy it. Alternatively, it can be downloaded from the Macromedia website at:

*   www.macromedia.com/software/fireworks

As well as downloading the full product, it is also possible to download a fully-functioning 30-day trial version from the same site.

 It is worth shopping around when buying a program such as Fireworks, because there can be considerable differences in price between different retailers. To find some online sellers of Fireworks, and other Macromedia products, go to their Web page at www.macromedia.com/uk/buy and click on the Find a Reseller button.

 The Macromedia Studio MX suite of programs (Dreamweaver, Fireworks, Flash and Freehand) can be ordered online at the Macromedia UK website for £589.

Click here to buy the full functioning version of Fireworks

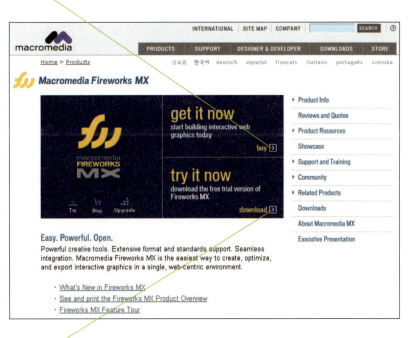

Click here to download the free 30-day trial version of Fireworks

Installing Fireworks

If Fireworks is downloaded from the Macromedia website it will be loaded automatically onto your computer. If you are using a CD-ROM version it should run automatically on a PC; on a Mac it is activated by double-clicking on the Fireworks installer icon. You will then be taken through the installation process and asked to enter information as required. Once the installation has been completed you may be asked to restart your computer.

System requirements

Windows

Once you have installed Fireworks, it is a good idea to add a shortcut (Windows) or an alias (Mac) to your desktop. This is done by locating the program file and right-clicking (Windows) or Ctrl+click (Mac) and dragging the icon onto the desktop. Release and select Create shortcut here (Windows) or Make Alias (Mac) from the menu.

- Windows 98 SE, Me, XP, 2000 or NT 4 (with Service Pack 6)

- 300 MhHz Intel Pentium II processor or better

- 64 MB of RAM (128 MB recommended)

- 80 MB of available disk space

- Adobe Type Manager 4 or later for use with Type 1 fonts

- 800 x 600 pixel resolution, 256-colour display (1024 x 768 resolution, 16 million colours recommended)

- CD-ROM drive

Mac

- Power Macintosh (G3 or higher recommended)

- OS 9.1 or later or version OS X 10.1 or later

- 64 MB of RAM (128 MB recommended)

- 80 MB of available disk space

- Adobe Type Manager 4 or later for use with Type 1 fonts

- 800 x 600 pixel resolution, 256-colour display (1024 x 768 resolution, 16 million colours recommended)

- CD-ROM drive

The first view

The Fireworks interface has been designed to match as closely as possible other Macromedia products such as Dreamweaver and Flash. This means you can switch between various programs, while remaining in a familiar environment. When Fireworks is first opened there is no document visible. To create a new document:

Select File>New from the Menu bar

Once a new document has been created a blank page will be visible in the Fireworks environment:

For more information on settings when creating new documents, see

The Fireworks panels can be accessed at any time by selecting Window from the Menu bar and then selecting the required panel. Each panel appears grouped with others that perform related or similar tasks.

page 18.

Preview tabs   Toolbar (Windows only)   Menu bar

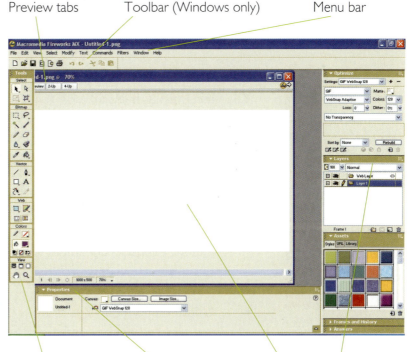

Close down any panels that you do not use regularly. If you have too many panels visible, this will mean there is less space for working in the document window.

Tools panel   Properties   Work area   Panels
                     Inspector

Menu bar and toolbars

Menu bar

The Menu bar is located at the top of the Fireworks screen and contains menus for accessing all of the functionality of the program. To view a menu, click on the relevant heading and then, if required, click on the arrow next to an option to view any sub-menus.

Toolbars (Windows only)

The Modify or Main toolbars are not available in the Mac version of Fireworks. These functions are available from the Menu bar, usually from the File or Edit menus.

For Windows, there are two toolbars available in Fireworks, the Main toolbar and the Modify toolbar. To access these:

From the Menu bar, select Window> Toolbars>Main/ Modify

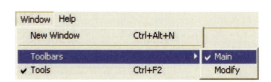

The functions on the Main toolbar are (from left to right):

The Undo function can be performed on numerous previous actions. The number of steps to which Undo can be applied can be set in the Preferences dialog box, which can be accessed by selecting Edit>Preferences (Windows) or Fireworks> Preferences (Mac) from the Menu bar.

- New. Creates a new document

- Open. Opens an existing document

- Save. Saves the currently active document

- Import. Imports a document from another format

- Export. Exports a document to another format

- Print. Prints the currently active document

- Undo. Undoes previous actions

- Redo. Replaces any actions that have been undone

- Cut. Removes a selection and copies it to the clipboard

- Copy. Copies a selection to the clipboard

- Paste. Pastes a selection that has been placed on the clipboard with either Cut or Copy

Tools panel

The Tools panel contains all of the most frequently used tools needed to create and edit graphics and images in Fireworks. Some of the buttons on the Tools panel have a small arrow at the bottom right-hand corner. By clicking on this a further selection of tools within this category can be selected. To access the full set of these options:

In Fireworks MX the Tools panel has been split into sections for bitmap and vector images. This means that you can select the relevant tool for the type of image without switching between bitmap and vector modes as with previous versions of Fireworks. This is known as modeless editing. For more information on bitmap and vector objects, see Chapter Two.

Click and hold here to access the full range of items available for a particular tool

The full range of default options on the Tools panel is:

The area underneath the tools on the tools panel is for selecting stroke and fill colours for objects. This is looked at in more detail in Chapter Three.

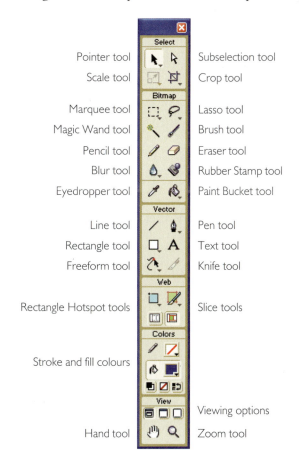

Pointer tool — Subselection tool
Scale tool — Crop tool
Marquee tool — Lasso tool
Magic Wand tool — Brush tool
Pencil tool — Eraser tool
Blur tool — Rubber Stamp tool
Eyedropper tool — Paint Bucket tool
Line tool — Pen tool
Rectangle tool — Text tool
Freeform tool — Knife tool
Rectangle Hotspot tools — Slice tools
Stroke and fill colours
Viewing options
Hand tool — Zoom tool

Additional options

The tools that have additional options are:

Pointer

Scale

*To see a
description of
what a
particular tool
does, roll the
cursor over it and wait a
couple of seconds for a box
describing the tool to appear.*

Crop

Lasso

Blur

Paint Bucket

Pen

Freeform

Marquee

Rectangle

Pointer tool (V, 0)
Select Behind tool (V, 0)

Scale tool (Q)
Skew tool (Q)
Distort tool (Q)

Crop tool (C)
Export Area tool (C)

Lasso tool (L)
Polygon Lasso tool (L)

Blur tool (R)
Sharpen tool (R)
Dodge tool (R)
Burn tool (R)
Smudge tool (R)

Paint Bucket tool (G)
Gradient tool (G)

Pen tool (P)
Vector Path tool (P)
Redraw Path tool (P)

Freeform tool (O)
Reshape Area tool (O)
Path Scrubber tool - additive
Path Scrubber tool - subtractive

Marquee tool (M)
Oval Marquee tool (M)

Rectangle tool (U)
Rounded Rectangle tool (U)
Ellipse tool (U)
Polygon tool (U)

Panels

Arranging panels

In order to be able to create, edit and manipulate objects, Fireworks provides a number of panels, each containing various devices for working with elements such as layers, frames and behaviors. Panels are grouped together in sets that perform similar functions. To work with panels:

Panels can be hidden by selecting Window from the Menu bar and clicking on any item that has a tick next to it.

1 Click here to move a panel set

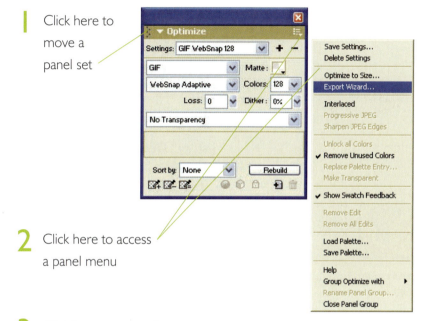

2 Click here to access a panel menu

The Properties Inspector has taken over the role of several panels in previous versions of Fireworks. These include the fill, stroke and effects panels, all of which can now be accessed from the Properties Inspector.

3 Click here to expand or collapse a panel

4 Click here to close a panel (Windows) or here (Mac)

Panels

A lot of the panels in previous versions of Fireworks have been consolidated in the Properties Inspector (see next page). However, there are still some individual panels, which can be accessed from the Window menu. Most of these are grouped within their own panel sets. The panels in Fireworks MX are:

Each panel will be dealt with in greater detail in the chapter to which their functions apply.

*   Optimize. This is used to change the file format of an image and also optimize it in terms of quality and file size

*   Layers. This is used to create images with different objects stacked on top of each other

*   Frames. This is used to create animated effects by placing images on individual frames

*   History. This displays the actions that have been performed on an image

*   Styles. This contains preset styles for applying to objects

URL stands for Uniform Resource Locator and is the unique address for individual Web pages.

*   Library. This is used to store objects that are reused several times within a document

*   URL. This is used to add a hyperlink (URL) to an object or part of an object

*   Color Mixer. This is used to create new colours

*   Swatches. This is used to select colours for the fill or stroke of an object

Usually when using panels, an object has to be selected first in the work area. The functions of a particular panel can then be applied to the selected object.

*   Info. This displays information about a selected object, such as its size and position

*   Behaviors. This is used to create effects for rollover images and popup menus

*   Find and Replace. This is used to replace elements within an image including text and colours

*   Project Log. This tracks changes made across several files

Properties Inspector

The Properties Inspector displays the attributes of the currently selected item on the page, whether it is a bitmap image, a vector object or a piece of text. In addition to viewing these attributes, they can also be altered by entering values within the Properties Inspector. For instance, if you want to change the size of an image, you can select it and then enter the new size that is required. To display the properties of a certain element it has to be selected first.

Always keep the Properties Inspector visible as it is the most commonly used element in Fireworks.

If an image has been opened but nothing has been selected, the Properties Inspector displays the image name and options for changing the size of the canvas and the image

The Properties Inspector is now a standardised feature across the MX suite of programs (Dreamweaver, Fireworks, Flash and Freehand). This means that the interface is familiar whichever program you are using.

If a bitmap image has been selected (or a bitmap tool), the Properties Inspector displays the image type and size or the relevant tool options

If a vector object has been selected (or a vector object tool), the Properties Inspector displays the options for applying effects to the fill and stroke of the object, or the relevant tool options

Creating files

When Fireworks opens, the work area is blank. You then have a choice of creating a new document or opening an existing one. Both new documents and existing ones are opened in PNG format, which is the proprietary file format used by Fireworks. Do not be put off by this: once you have created or opened a document you can then save it in numerous other formats. This is known as exporting a document. Once this has been done, a new file is created in the specified format and the original Fireworks document remains.

If you want to create a new document there are a few options that can be specified first:

PNG stands for Portable Network Graphic, which is a file format that can be used on the Web, although it has not gained such general popularity as GIFs or JPEGs.

1 Select File>New from the Menu bar

The canvas is the area on which you add content to your Fireworks documents. By default, it is white, but it can be made transparent or specified as a particular colour. If you specify a colour, this will appear behind any part of the canvas that has not had content added to it.

2 Enter values for the width, height and resolution of the new document

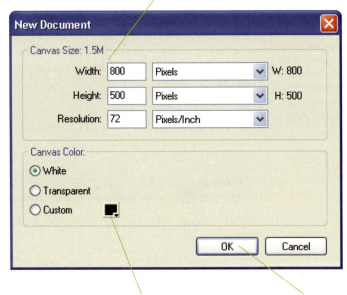

If you want to create a new file with an image you have copied from another application, the size of the canvas is automatically amended to the size of the image to be pasted.

3 Select a colour for the canvas i.e. the background

4 Click OK

Opening files

Files created in formats other than PNG can be opened in Fireworks. However, when they are opened, they are done so in PNG format. To open existing files:

When an existing image is opened in Fireworks, the canvas is created at the exact same size as the image that is being opened. If you want to change the canvas size at any point of editing a document, select Modify>Canvas>Canvas Size from the Menu bar and enter the required values for the height and width of the canvas. It can also be altered from the Properties Inspector, as long as the image itself is not selected.

1 Select File>Open from the Menu bar

2 Select the file you want to open, from your file structure.

3 Click Open

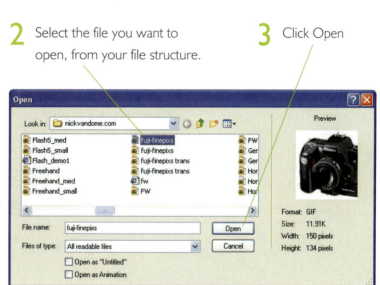

When a file from a format other than PNG is opened, the original file remains the same – the one opened in Fireworks is just a PNG copy of the original.

4 The file opens in the Fireworks work area. This is in PNG format, which is denoted by the icon here

Importing files

When you are working with a program such as Fireworks, there will probably be frequent occasions when you want to combine more than one image. This can be done to create montages, or simply to insert an element from one image into another. This is done by importing an image into an existing one. To do this:

1 Make sure an image is already open and select File>Import from the Menu bar

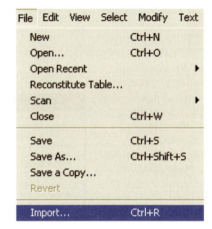

- GIF

- JPEG

- TIFF

- BMP

- Targa

- EPS

- FH or FT (Freehand)

- PSD (Photoshop)

- AI or ART (Illustrator)

- CDR (CorelDraw)

2 Select a file

3 Select a file format

4 Click Open

...cont'd

It is also possible to import images from scanners and digital cameras, as long as you have the relevant devices and drivers (software). For a scanner, select File>Scan and select the device. For a digital camera, select File>Import and select the device.

When separate layers are used, items on each layer can be edited independently of each other. In addition, layers can also be merged or blended together. For more on working with layers, see Chapter Seven.

5 Click once with the cursor to insert the image

6 The imported image is placed on a new layer on top of the existing one

Saving files

Since Fireworks uses a variety of different file formats, there are also different choices for saving files, once they have been edited:

Save

The standard Save function can be used to save documents into the Fireworks proprietary file format, '–.png'. To do this:

1 Select File>Save from the Menu bar

If you want to save a Fireworks document in a format other than PNG then this cannot be done with the Save or Save As function. The Export function has to be used instead, see next page.

2 Select a location in which to save the file and click Save. The only option available in the Save as type box is PNG

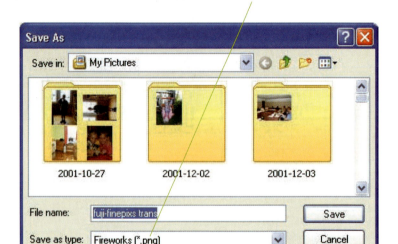

Save As can also be used to save a file for the first time. In this respect it operates in the same way as the Save function.

Save As

This is similar to Save, except that it can be used to make a copy of an existing PNG file. This is accessed by selecting File>Save As from the Menu bar. By default, the document will be given the same name as the original and a warning dialog box will appear asking if you want to copy over the existing file. If you do, select Yes, if not give the file a different name.

Save a Copy

This is similar to the Save As function.

The concept of exporting can seem a little daunting at first but it is a function that is used frequently in Fireworks. Think of it as saving files.

Exporting

Both files that are created in Fireworks, and those that have been opened from another file format, can be exported. This means they are saved in a file format other than PNG. This format can be specified before the file is exported. To export a file:

1 Select File>Export Preview from the Menu bar

2 Click here to set the default Export format. (This will be used for all other files that are exported, unless specified otherwise)

If you know what the current Export settings are, the Export Preview step can be skipped. Instead, select File>Export from the Menu bar and select a location into which to save the file.

3 Click Export

4 Give the file a name

For a standard image the 'Save as type' box in the Export dialog box can be left at Images Only. When using items such as rollovers, slices and hotspots, this requires a different setting and these issues are looked at in Chapters Eight and Nine.

5 Click Save

Getting help

Fireworks Help

This provides an online guide to all aspects of the program:

Select Help>Using Fireworks from the Menu bar

Click here to access the Help contents and index

The Help menu also has links to online Fireworks resources such as Fireworks Forums and the Fireworks Support Center.

Click here to access topics

The selected topic appears here

Answers panel

The Answers panel (select Window>Answers from the Menu bar) provides access to a variety of help topics, including latest updates from the Macromedia website.

The Help menu also enables you to register your copy of Fireworks online. This entitles you to news about upgrades, technical support and the latest Fireworks news.

1 Click here to access help topics

2 Click here to access online updates

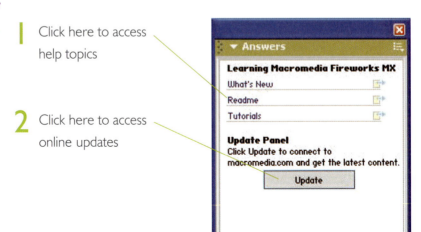

Working with objects and images

Either bitmap or vector images can be used in Fireworks. This chapter explains the difference between the two and discusses some of the issues connected with working with both types. It also shows some editing techniques that can be applied to images.

Covers

Bitmaps | 26

Vectors | 27

Identifying selected items | 28

Points and paths | 29

Working with paths | 30

Resizing images | 31

Image editing | 32

Image retouching | 33

Chapter Two

Bitmaps

About bitmaps

Fireworks can be used to create and edit two types of image files: bitmaps and vector images. Bitmaps are images that are made up of physical dots of colour, known as pixels. In this respect, bitmaps can be thought of as 'real' images. However, bitmaps have some limitations:

The overall size of a bitmap depends on the amount of colour information stored within each pixel. This can vary from 8 bits to 24 bits. Bitmaps in 24-bit colour are much bigger in size.

- They tend to result in larger file sizes than their vector counterparts

- They usually suffer from a deterioration in quality when they are resized. This is because each individual pixel has to expand or contract to make an image larger or smaller. This is particularly noticeable when an image is increased in size, since each pixel has to cover a greater area

Bitmap images appear most commonly in the form of digital photographs.

Fireworks MX offers modeless editing, which means that you only have to select an editing tool from the tools panels, rather than having to switch between bitmap and vector mode. If the type of tool is not appropriate for the image mode then you will not be able to use that tool.

A range of editing functions can be applied to bitmaps including recolouring, cloning, cropping and blurring. Some of the tools in the tools panel can only be used on bitmaps, but vector objects, such as rectangles and circles, can be added to bitmap images.

Bitmaps appear most commonly as photographic images

Working with objects and images

Either bitmap or vector images can be used in Fireworks. This chapter explains the difference between the two and discusses some of the issues connected with working with both types. It also shows some editing techniques that can be applied to images.

Covers

Bitmaps | 26

Vectors | 27

Identifying selected items | 28

Points and paths | 29

Working with paths | 30

Resizing images | 31

Image editing | 32

Image retouching | 33

Chapter Two

Bitmaps

About bitmaps

Fireworks can be used to create and edit two types of image files: bitmaps and vector images. Bitmaps are images that are made up of physical dots of colour, known as pixels. In this respect, bitmaps can be thought of as 'real' images. However, bitmaps have some limitations:

- They tend to result in larger file sizes than their vector counterparts

- They usually suffer from a deterioration in quality when they are resized. This is because each individual pixel has to expand or contract to make an image larger or smaller. This is particularly noticeable when an image is increased in size, since each pixel has to cover a greater area

Bitmap images appear most commonly in the form of digital photographs.

A range of editing functions can be applied to bitmaps including recolouring, cloning, cropping and blurring. Some of the tools in the tools panel can only be used on bitmaps, but vector objects, such as rectangles and circles, can be added to bitmap images.

The overall size of a bitmap depends on the amount of colour information stored within each pixel. This can vary from 8 bits to 24 bits. Bitmaps in 24-bit colour are much bigger in size.

Fireworks MX offers modeless editing, which means that you only have to select an editing tool from the tools panels, rather than having to switch between bitmap and vector mode. If the type of tool is not appropriate for the image mode then you will not be able to use that tool.

Bitmaps appear most commonly as photographic images

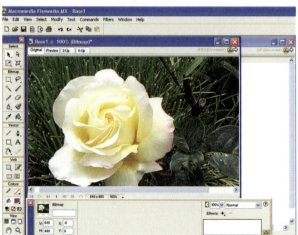

Vectors

Vector images are created from mathematical equations rather than physical pixels of colour. However, this does not mean they are limited in what you can do with them and the types of items that can be created. Lines, fills, colours, textures and text can all be created with vectors, as can more complex items such as rollover images, hotspots and sliced images.

The two main advantages of vector images are:

- Since they are based on a mathematical equation rather than a physical object, they create files that are much smaller in size than their bitmap counterparts. This is an important consideration when designing items for use on a website

- It is possible to resize vector images without losing any image quality. This is because the resized image relies on a newly created mathematical equation rather than stretching pixels. This gives much greater flexibility to designers

Vectors can be used to design entire websites and they are an excellent option for items such as Web graphics, navigation bars or buttons.

Vector images can be created using items such as fills, lines and text:

Rollover images are ones that change appearance when the cursor is moved over them on a Web page. Hotspots are images that have hyperlinks assigned to particular parts of them. Slices are images that are broken (or sliced) into smaller parts. The whole image can then be recreated on a Web page by re-assembling the slices of the image.

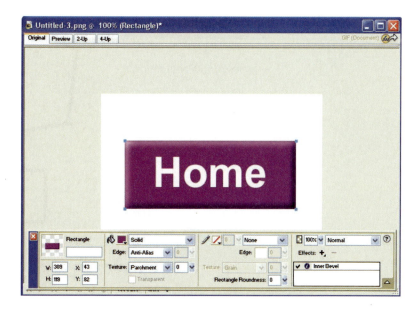

Identifying selected items

When working with both vectors and bitmaps it is important to know when particular items are selected.

Identifying vector selections

Vector items can be identified by thin lines around their border. When an object is selected this is light-blue. When you pass the cursor over a vector object that is not selected, the border appears red, to show the boundaries of the object even though it is not selected.

The blue border around a vector object denotes its path and points. For more information on this, see the next page.

To select a vector object, click on it once with the Pointer tool. A light-blue border will appear around the object, with small rectangles at the points where a border changes direction

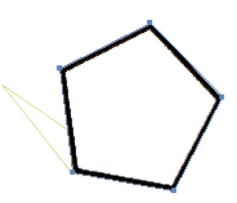

To select numerous vector objects, hold down the Shift key and click on each item in turn

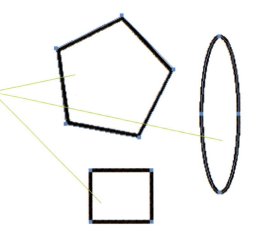

Points and paths

Since vectors are based on mathematical calculations, they have clearly defined paths and points as items of reference. A path is a line, which may be straight or curved, made up of straight line segments and points when the path changes direction. Points are denoted by small rectangles on an object's path. A path can be as simple or as complicated as you want:

When separate paths are created, they are done so on different layers. However, it is possible to combine different paths. To do this, select the paths you want to combine by holding down Shift and clicking on each path (even when they are on separate layers this should select them all). Select Modify>Combine Paths>Join from the Menu bar to create a composite path. Paths can be overlapping to do this, but they do not have to be.

A simple path: a straight line between two points

A more complex path, with points occurring whenever there is a change in direction of the path

Vector paths can be grouped as a single element. This places a rectangular border around the path and it then operates like a single element. To do this, select a vector path and select Modify>Group from the Menu bar

Working with paths

In vector mode there is a great deal of flexibility for working with objects created with paths. It is possible to reshape them, resize them and move them, using the Pointer and the Subselection tools.

Reshaping vectors

When reshaping vectors, the Subselection tool works in a similar way to the Pen tool. For more information about this, see Chapter Four.

Select the Subselection tool and select a vector object by clicking on it once

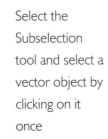

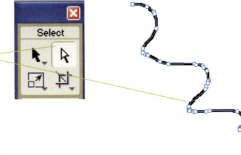

The Freeform tool can also be used to reshape vector objects. This can be used to create a more curved appearance.

2 Click and drag a point to reshape the object

Moving vectors

With the Subselection tool, click and drag on a path

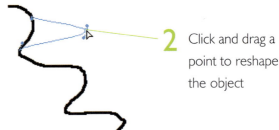

With the Pointer tool, click and drag anywhere on the vector object

Resizing images

Resizing an entire image is not the same as resizing individual elements within it. It is best to resize the whole image once you have finished all of the editing tasks that you need to perform on it.

When working with images in Fireworks there will be plenty of occasions when you will want to edit the overall size of an image. This may be to ensure it fits properly on a Web page, or for printing a hard copy. This may be particularly useful if you are printing photographs. To do this:

1 Select Modify>Canvas>Trim Canvas from the Menu bar. This reduces the background to the widest points of the image

Even vector images are calculated in pixels when it comes to the overall image size.

2 Select Modify>Canvas>Image Size from the Menu bar

3 Enter values here to change the size of the image

Check the Resample Image box if you want pixels to be added when you increase the size of the image. This is educated guesswork that tries to ensure that image quality is maintained.

4 Enter values here for a specific print size

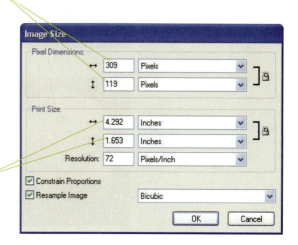

5 Click OK

Image editing

Fireworks has some functions for enhancing photographic images. These have been expanded in Fireworks MX so that there is now a wider range of filters and effects that can be applied to photographic images.

Adjusting colour

Select Filters>Adjust Color from the Menu bar and select the effect you want to apply.

The Auto Levels command can be used to edit images by adjusting the colour elements in relation to the lightest and darkest points. However, this can be a bit hit and miss so be prepared to use the Undo button if you do not like the end result.

Some simple effects can be achieved and also some more surreal ones

Original

Brightness and Contrast

Experiment with different combinations of brightness and contrast and hue and saturation to see what kind of effects can be achieved. When you are working with images you may not always want to use realistic effects.

Hue and Saturation

Invert

Image retouching

Blurring and sharpening

Blurring can be used to give an image a soft focus effect, while sharpening can be used to give a crisper appearance to an image that appears slightly out of focus. Both of these have different options that can be selected, which vary the amount of the effect that is applied. To use blurring and sharpening:

 Specific areas of an image can have blurring or sharpening applied to them, while leaving the rest of the image untouched. To do this, select an area with the Marquee or the Lasso tools and then apply the required effect to the selected area.

Select Filters>Blur (or Sharpen) from the Menu bar and then select the amount of the effect that you want to apply

Blurring can give a softer appearance to an image. It can also be used to create the impression of speed by blurring the background behind a vehicle such as a sports car

 Options such as blurring and sharpening can also be accessed from the Tools panel. Also included are the Dodge, Burn and Smudge tools, which can be used to alter the appearance of images. The Dodge tool can be used to lighten dark areas of an image and the Burn tool can be used to darken light areas.

Sharpening (or Sharpen More) emphasises the lines between different colours in an image which can be used to make a blurred image appear more in focus

Eye Candy

This can be used to add weird and wonderful special effects to an image. It can be applied to a whole image or a selection within an image:

Select
Filters>Eye
Candy from
the Menu bar.
Preview the
effect and click
here to buy
the full range

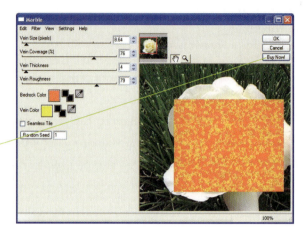

Elements such as Eye Candy and Alien Skin Splat are created by third party developers rather than Macromedia.

Alien Skin Splat

These are similar effects to Eye Candy and the full range can be bought online by clicking the Buy Now button in the Alien Skin Splat dialog box. The sample effect is to change the edges of an image:

Select Filters>
Alien Skin Splat
from the Menu
bar. The sample
effect can be used
to change the
edges of an image

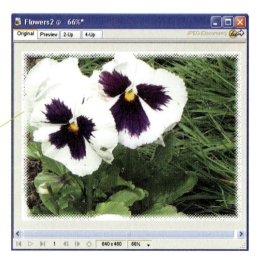

Creating objects

Fireworks has an extensive array of options available for creating graphical objects. This chapter shows how to use some of the drawing tools and it also details the panels that can be used to edit and enhance objects.

Covers

Drawing modifiers | 36

Drawing tools | 37

Adding text | 40

Viewing objects | 41

Adding fills | 42

Adding strokes | 44

Adding effects | 45

Styles panel | 47

Color Mixer panel | 48

Chapter Three

Drawing modifiers

Objects are created in Fireworks by using the drawing tools in the Tools panel. This chapter will look specifically at the tools that are used for creating objects, while the next chapter will cover those that are used to edit existing objects.

For all of the tools used to create objects, modifiers can be accessed to specify fill and stroke colours. This can either be done before the object is created or it can be used to edit the stroke and fill colour of an existing object. The modifiers are located underneath the tools on the Tools panel:

Stroke and fill colours can also be selected and mixed in the Swatches and Mixer panels and also in the Properties Inspector.

The default colours are black for stroke and white for fill. These can be amended by selecting Edit>Preferences (Windows) or Fireworks>Preferences (Mac) from the Menu bar and changing the required settings under the General tab.

Click here to access the colour palette for the stroke colour

Click here to access the colour palette for the fill colour

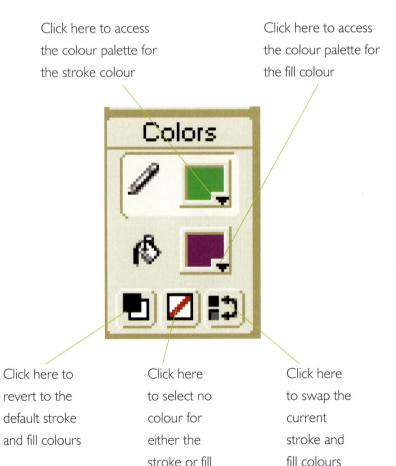

Click here to revert to the default stroke and fill colours

Click here to select no colour for either the stroke or fill

Click here to swap the current stroke and fill colours

Drawing tools

Rectangle set

The tools that appear with the Rectangle tool as the default are the ones to use if you want to create geometric shapes such as squares and circles. Each tool is used to create objects by selecting it from the Tools panel and then clicking and dragging in the work area. Objects will be created with the currently selected stroke and fill attributes. These tools are:

Rectangle tool   Rounded Rectangle tool

To draw a perfect circle or square select the Ellipse (or Rectangle) tool and hold down the Shift key while drawing the object.

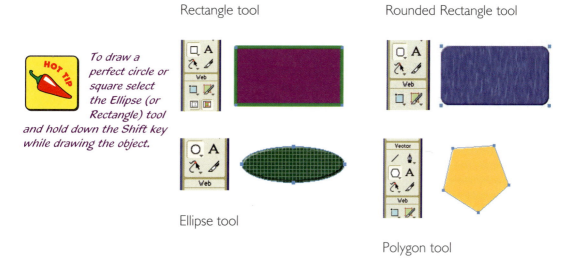

Ellipse tool

Polygon tool

When using the Rounded Rectangle tool the degree of roundness can be altered in the Properties Inspector:

Click here and drag the slider to change the amount of roundness for the corners of a rectangle

Pen tool

This is used to create lines and items called Bezier curves, which are shapes created based on mathematical formulae. It can also be used to create shapes in a similar way to producing a dot-to-dot picture. To create straight-lined objects with the Pen tool:

Objects created with the Pen tool can be edited with the Subselection tool.

1 Select the Pen tool and click once on the work area. This is the start point of the object

2 Click on another point to create a straight line

3 Continue with this technique and click back on the start point to create an enclosed object

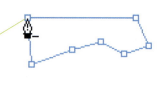

You can add new points to an existing path by using the Pen tool. To do this, click once anywhere on a path where there is not already a point.

To create a curved object:

1 Select the Pen tool and click and drag to create a line

2 Click and drag to add curves or click once for straight lines

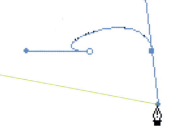

Line tool

This is used to draw straight lines.

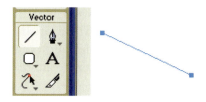

Objects created with the Line, Pencil and Brush tools are vector items and can be edited accordingly.

Pencil tool

This is used to draw freehand lines.

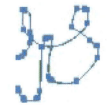

Brush tool

This is used to create the effect of lines drawn with a large paintbrush.

To use the Paint Bucket tool, click once on it on the Tools panel, select a fill colour and then click once inside the object whose fill you want to edit. The whole area will then be filled with the specified fill colour.

Paint Bucket tool

This is used to add or change the fill colour of an object.

Adding text

When creating objects, text can be as important an element as colour or shape. Text can be used with images for items such as headings, captions and labels for buttons on a Web page. To add text to an image:

Positioning text is one function where it is useful to zoom in on the element being positioned. This will allow for greater accuracy. If you are having trouble positioning it exactly where you want, select View>Grid from the Menu bar and make sure that Snap to Grid is deselected.

1 Select the Text tool from the Tools panel

2 Click once on the canvas. This will activate the text Properties Inspector and insert a text box on the canvas

Once an image has been exported into a format other than PNG it is not then possible to edit text boxes independently from the rest of the image.

3 Select formatting options in the Properties Inspector and enter text

Click here to select font   Click here to select size   Click here to select colour   Click here to select formatting

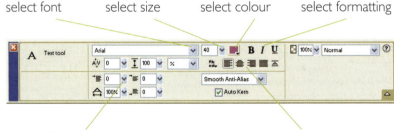

Text can be edited by clicking on it with the text tool directly on the canvas.

Click here to select spacing

Click here to select alignment

Viewing objects

When creating and editing objects, it is useful to be able to view them at different magnifications. For instance, you may want to zoom in to edit a small part of an object and then view the whole of the object within one screen. There are several ways to do this:

Click and drag with the Zoom tool to magnify a selected part of an image.

Zoom tool

Select the Zoom tool and click once to increase the magnification. This goes as high as 6400%

Magnification can be decreased by selecting the Zoom tool,
holding down the Alt key and clicking within the work area.

Menu bar

Select View > Magnification and the required magnification setting

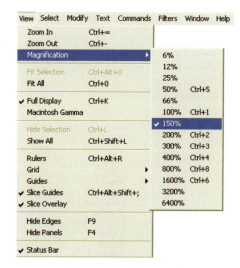

When working with images it is always a good idea to zoom in to
certain areas to make sure it is exactly as intended. This is particularly important for items such as straight lines that have to join exactly.

Document window

Click here next to the status bar at the bottom of the open window to access the magnification menu as above

Adding fills

When working with objects, the Properties Inspector can be used to add fill colours and patterns. This gives greater flexibility than the standard fill colours that can be selected from the Tools panel. To add fills using the Properties Inspector:

It is perfectly acceptable to use solid colours for the fill of objects, and there will be times when this is preferable to more artistic designs.

1 Select an object or a drawing tool such as the Rectangle tool. The currently selected solid fill colour is displayed here in the Properties Inspector

You can change the solid colour selection in the Properties Inspector by clicking on the colour box. The new colour will then also be the one in the fill box on the Tools panel.

2 Click here to access the menu for fill patterns or gradient fills

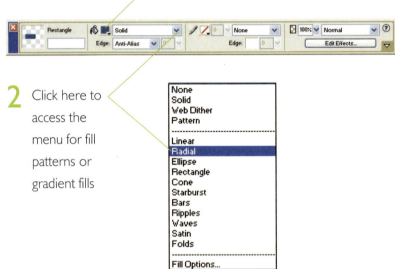

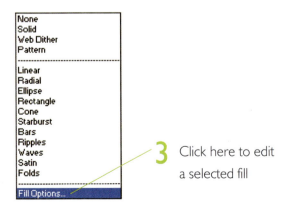

3 Click here to edit a selected fill

Anti-alias edges give a smoother appearance to the edges of objects. This is particularly effective for items such as circles or ovals. The Hard option creates a straighter, but less forgiving, edge and is better suited to items such as rectangles and squares. The feather option creates a blurred effect around the edges. The level of this can be altered (i.e. more or less of the edge area can be blurred) and it is a good option if you want to blend the object into the background.

4 Click here to edit the selected gradient fill

5 Click here to select a style for the edges of the fill

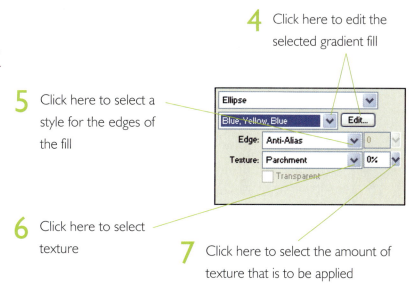

6 Click here to select texture

7 Click here to select the amount of texture that is to be applied

Some examples of how the fills can be used on objects:

Ellipse fill, copper gradient, anti-alias edges and Chiffon texture at 50%

Starburst fill, pastels gradient, feather edges and Confetti texture at 80%

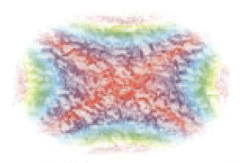

Adding strokes

The Properties Inspector can be used to add colours and textures to strokes. To edit strokes using the Properties Inspector:

1 Select the stroke of an object (or an individual stroke such as a line) and click here on the Properties Inspector

The stroke colour and width can be edited by clicking on the two boxes to the right of the pencil icon on the Properties Inspector. The width is increased or decreased by dragging a slider.

2 Select an option from the stroke menu

3 Click here to edit the selected stroke

An object has to be selected for the attributes of the stroke to be displayed in the Properties Inspector.

4 Drag here to set the softness or hardness of the edges of the stroke

5 Click here to select the width of the stroke

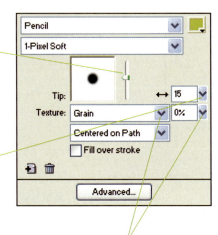

6 Click here to select the texture of the stroke and the amount to be applied

Adding effects

The effect options on the Properties Inspector can be used to further refine the appearance of objects:

Effect settings

The subtle use of effects such as embossing and bevelling can produce stylish buttons and graphics for use on Web pages.

1 Select an object

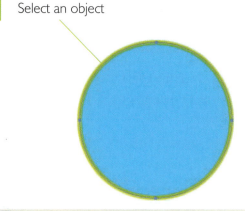

Several effects can be applied to the same item.

2 Click here to select the Effects menu

Effects are only applied to the currently selected item. If you then create a new object, this will just have the currently selected stroke and fill attributes applied to it, not any effects.

3 Select an effect from the Effects menu

4 Each effect has a options box that can be used to modify the attributes of the effect

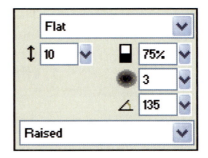

5 Once the effect has been selected it is added to the Effects box on the Properties Inspector

Several different effects can be added to a single object.

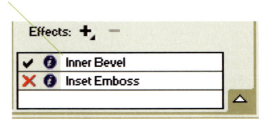

Saving effects as style

Once an effect has been created it can be saved as a style and it will then appear in the Styles panel. To do this:

1 Create an effect and select Options>Save as Style from the Effects Menu bar (see Step 3 on previous page)

2 Give the style a name and click OK to add it to the Styles panel

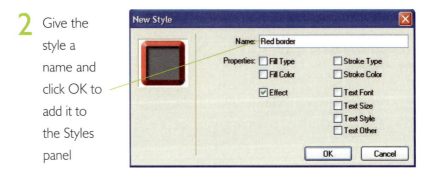

Styles panel

For the designer who does not want to have to go to the trouble of creating his or her own designs, there is a useful Styles panel of pre-designed fills and strokes. These can be applied to objects and also text:

A style from the Styles panel will over-write any previously selected fill or stroke attributes.

1 Select Window>Styles from the Menu bar to access the Styles panel

2 Select an object and click here to apply a pre-set style

Existing styles can be edited by double-clicking on them in the Styles panel and then changing their attributes in the Edit Style dialog box.

3 Select a text box and click here to apply a pre-set text style

Text styles can be used to good effect for items such as headings or sub-headings, but only if they are used sparingly.

4 Click here to create your own custom styles

Color Mixer panel

The Color Mixer panel can be used to create your own custom colours, in addition to the ones in the standard colour palette. To use the Color Mixer panel:

1 Select Window>Color Mixer from the Menu bar to access the Color Mixer panel

If you create your own colour it may not be one of the 256 Web-safe colours that appear the same on all Web browsers. This may mean that the colour you have specified will not appear consistently across different browsers.

2 Select either the stroke or the fill option

3 Click here to select a colour from the colour palette

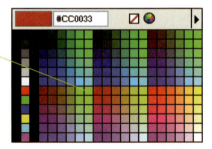

4 Click here to select a custom colour

A hexadecimal colour is one where the levels of red, green and blue are each determined by a two-digit code.

5 Enter values here to specify a colour through a hexadecimal code

Editing objects

Once objects have been created it is possible to apply a variety of editing techniques to them. This provides enormous flexibility for creative design. This chapter looks at some of the tools that can be used for editing objects and some of the effects that can be achieved.

Covers

Reshaping | 50

Orientation | 52

Scaling | 54

Skewing | 55

Distorting | 56

Arranging and aligning | 57

Selecting parts of objects | 58

Cropping | 61

Cloning | 62

Erasing | 63

Selecting colours | 64

Chapter Four

Reshaping

One of the most powerful object editing functions in Fireworks is the ability to reshape vector objects. This is done through the use of several tools:

Subselection tool

Select the Subselection tool and click and drag on a point to stretch the object at that point

Click on a point and click and drag on a handle to distort the object

When a path is selected with the Subselection tool a hollow square indicates a point. When this is selected, solid squares appear along a line that goes through the point. These are known as point handles and can be used to edit an object.

Freeform tool

Select the Freeform tool. Move it over a point until a small S shape appears next to it. Use this to drag and distort the object around this point

If the Freeform tool is clicked within an object and then dragged outwards, this will expand the fill in the direction the tool is moved.

Move the Freeform tool towards a path, until a small circle appears next to the cursor. Click and push to distort the object inwards

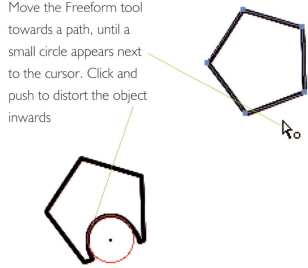

By default, the Reshape Area tool is not selected. If this is the case, click on the black triangle next to the Freeform tool and then select the Reshape Area tool that appears.

Reshape Area tool

Select the Reshape Area tool. Click and push to reshape an object, in a similar way to pushing sand with a cup

The size of the Reshape Area tool and the pressure with which it pushes the fill are determined in the Properties Inspector, in the Size and Strength boxes.

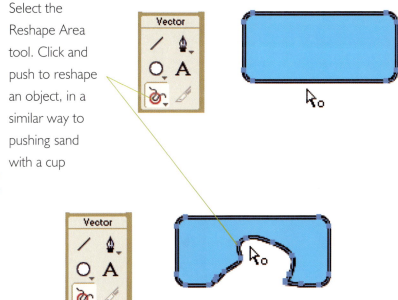

Orientation

Once an object has been created it is useful to be able to change its orientation i.e. rotate it by varying degrees on the canvas. There are several options for doing this:

Scale tool

This can be used to rotate an object manually:

1 Select an object and select the Scale tool from the Tools panel

  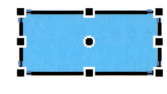

The other tools grouped with the Scale tool, i.e. the Distort and the Skew tools can also be used to rotate an object.

2 Click anywhere on the canvas until the circular arrowhead appears

 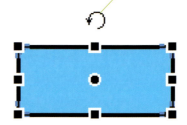

To rotate the whole canvas, select Modify> Canvas from the Menu bar and select the appropriate rotation option. This can be used for items such as photographs that appear on their sides or upside down.

3 Drag to rotate the object

 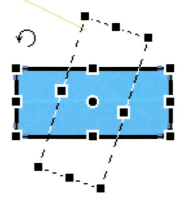

Numeric Transform

1   Select an object and select Modify>Transform>Numeric Transform from the Menu bar

The Free Transform option on the Transform menu works in the same way as rotating an object with the tools on the previous page.

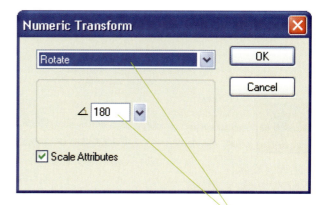

2   In the Numeric Transform dialog box, select Rotate here and enter the amount you want the object to rotate

Preset Transform

The options on the Transform menu can also be used to rotate an object by a specific angle:

The Flip Horizontal and Flip Vertical options are useful if you want to create a mirror image of an object. It is also useful if you want to make an object face the opposite direction.

Select an object and select one of the options from the Transform menu

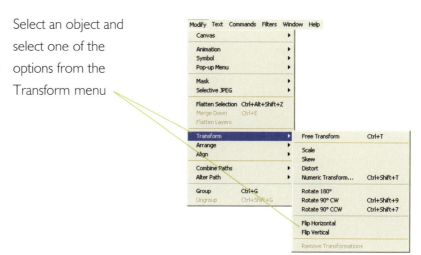

Scaling

When working with objects, designers frequently need to change the size of them. This can be done with the Scale tool:

1 Select an object and select the Scale tool on the Tools panel

The Scale option can also be accessed from the Menu bar, by selecting Modify>Transform>Scale. This is also the case for the Skew and the Distort options (see next two pages).

2 Click and drag here to change the horizontal size of the object

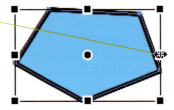

To scale an object to a specific value, select Modify>Transform>Numeric Transform from the Menu bar. Make sure Scale is selected in the top box and then enter values in the boxes below for the new scale size.

3 Click and drag here to change the vertical size of the object

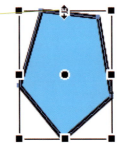

4 Click and drag here to change the horizontal and vertical size of the object. This is done in proportion

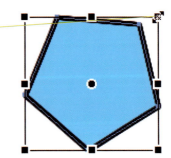

Skewing

Skewing can be used to change the shape of an object. It is particularly effective for creating a sense of perspective.

I Select an object and select the Skew tool on the Tools panel

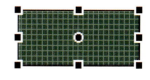

Skewing can be used to achieve creative effects with photographic images. However, do not overapply this effect, otherwise the photograph may become unrecognisable.

2 Click and drag here to skew the horizontal axis of the object

3 Click and drag here to skew the vertical axis of the object

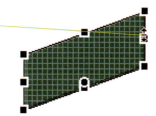

To achieve a sense of distance with an object, skew the top horizontal axis inwards. This will make the object the widest at the bottom, giving the effect that it is disappearing into the distance.

4 Click and drag here to skew one side of the object

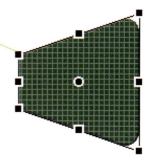

Distorting

1 Select an object and select the Distort tool on the Tools panel

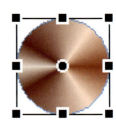

2 Click and drag here to distort the horizontal axis of the object

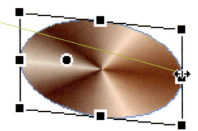

If you try and distort an object by dragging a corner handle over and beyond its opposite side, you will not be able to do so.

3 Click and drag here to distort the vertical axis of the object

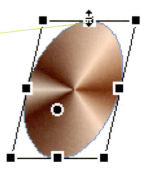

4 Click and drag here to distort the two sides next to this point

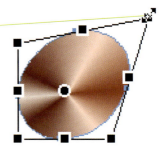

Arranging and aligning

If you are working with several objects on the same layer you will soon find that you want to place certain objects, or parts of objects, above or below others. This is known as the stacking order. For instance, you may want to create an image of a person sitting behind a table, in which case the table will be above the person in the stacking order. To arrange objects:

If you want to send an item behind other objects the commands are the same in reverse: Send Backward sends an object behind the item immediately behind it; Send to Back sends it behind all of the items below it i.e. it goes to the bottom of the stacking order.

1 Create three objects and overlap them all. Select the bottom object

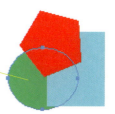

2 Select Modify > Arrange > Bring to Front. This brings the object above all of the items above it

When working with elements such as buttons for a Web page it is necessary to be able to align them either horizontally or vertically. This can be done manually by using the Fireworks grid and dragging them into place. However a much more efficient way is to use the Align options:

If you are designing a series of buttons for a navigation bar on a Web page, align them according to where you are going to place the navigation bar i.e. left if it is going to be on the left of the page, top if it is going to be at the top and so on.

1 Select two or more objects

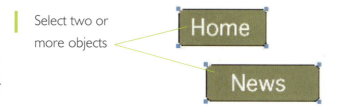

2 Select Modify > Align from the Menu bar and select one of the options

Selecting parts of objects

There are three tools that can be used to select parts of objects, rather than entire objects. These are the Marquee tool, the Lasso tool and the Magic Wand tool.

Marquee tool

There are two choices of Marquee tool, the rectangular Marquee tool, (which is just known as the Marquee tool) and the Oval Marquee tool. Both operate in the same way:

Hold down the Shift key when using the Marquee tools to create an exactly square or circular selection.

1 Select one of the Marquee tools

2 Select an area on an object by clicking and dragging. This has to be a bitmap object rather than a vector one

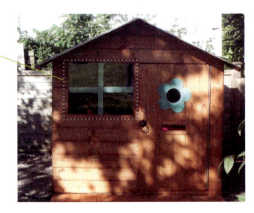

Once you have selected an area of an object it is then possible to feather it i.e. give it blurred edges. This can be put to good effect for softening the edges around items such as photographs. To do this, make a selection and select Select>Feather from the Menu bar and enter a value for the amount of feathering you want to apply.

3 Once an area has been selected it can then be edited independently. This can include dragging the selection away from the original object, or editing its fill and stroke attributes

Lasso tool

The Lasso tool, and its grouped tools, can be used to make irregular selections, rather than symmetrical ones:

One effective use for the Lasso tool is for selecting red eyes in photographic images. These can then be edited by applying a more appropriate colour.

1 Select the Lasso tool

2 Make a freehand selection on an object

As with the Marquee tools, Lasso selections can only be made on bitmap images.

3 Edit the selection as appropriate

Polygon Lasso tool

This can be used to make a 'dot-to-dot' selection:

1 Select the Polygon Lasso tool

2 Make the selection by clicking once at each point around the object you want included

The Magic Wand tool is a good option if you want to select an irregular area of a particular colour, without having to use the Lasso tools.

Magic Wand tool

The Magic Wand tool can be used to select areas of the same, or similar, colour. Its attributes can be set to vary the range of colours that are selected. To select an area with the Magic Wand tool:

1 Select the Magic Wand tool

The Magic Wand tool works by selecting similarly coloured pixels to the one that is first selected. The level of tolerance dictates the divergence in colour that is allowed between pixels. So if the tolerance is set to a low value, e.g. 10, only very similarly coloured pixels will be selected. At a high tolerance, such as 80, a much wider range of pixels will be selected and so the overall selection will be bigger.

2 Enter a Tolerance value in the Properties Inspector

3 Click once on an area to select it

Tolerance at 10

Tolerance at 80

To deselect an area that has been selected with the Magic Wand tool, click on it again with the same tool.

Cropping

Cropping is a technique that is most frequently used in connection with photographic images. Even the best photographers do not always capture images exactly as they want them and cropping can be used to remove the unwanted area behind the main subject of an image. To crop an image:

1 Select the Crop tool

Cropping should always be considered in connection with images of people, since these often contain background areas that are unnecessary and distracting. Try to remove as much of this as possible so that there is as little as possible to detract from the main subject of the image.

2 Click and drag around the area of the image that you want to retain

3 If necessary, edit the selection by dragging the resizing handles

Cropping not only improves the visual appearance of images, it also reduces the file size, which decreases their downloading time over the Web.

4 Press Return or Enter to crop the image so that only the selected area is visible

Cloning

Cloning is one of the reasons why digital images should never be fully trusted. This technique enables you to copy or remove elements of a photograph, or graphic, to a standard that makes it look like an original. For instance, it is possible to remove individuals or unwanted objects from a photograph, or copy existing ones so that they are perfectly duplicated. In Fireworks, this is done with the Rubber Stamp tool:

Cloning is a good option if you have text on an object that you want to change (this is once an image has been exported and the text has become part of the image rather than an individual text block.) Use the Rubber Stamp tool to cover over the text, then add a new text block and save the image as a PNG or export it again.

1 Select the Rubber Stamp tool

2 Hold down Alt and click on a part of the image that you want to use as the starting point for cloning. A circle with a blue outline will appear

If you are removing an item in a photographic image, you will need to move the cloning point several times in order to create a seamless finished product.

3 Drag the cursor over the item to be removed. As the blue circle moves over the image in tandem with the cursor, the area in the circle will be copied at the point where the cursor is

Erasing

The Eraser tool can be used to remove areas of a bitmap object, or give them varying degrees of opacity. To do this:

1 Select a bitmap object and select the Eraser tool

2 Select the Eraser tool options in the Properties Inspector

Click here to select the size of the tip

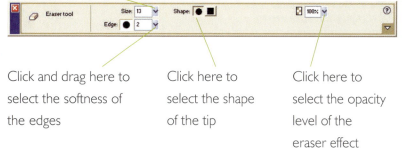

Click and drag here to select the softness of the edges

Click here to select the shape of the tip

Click here to select the opacity level of the eraser effect

3 Click and drag to remove elements from an image

Selecting colours

If you want to reuse a particular colour that appears in an existing object, but you are unsure about making an exact match, the Eyedropper tool can be used to copy it into one of the colour palettes. To do this:

If you want to copy something like skin-tone colours, the Eyedropper tool is not the best option to choose. This is because it only picks up a singe colour and when this is reapplied it is done so as a continuous tone. If this is then used to recolour someone's face, they will end up looking very two-dimensional. A better option in this instance is to clone one area to another, as shown on page 62.

1 Select the Eyedropper tool

2 Click once on the colour that you want to copy. This will then appear as the default for either the stroke or the fill colour

3 Click on the colour box for the colour you have selected

4 Click here to access the Color dialog box

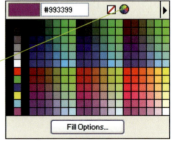

In Windows when a colour has been added as a Custom Color it will not be available in the standard colour palettes. To access it you have to access the Color dialog box as in Step 4 and then select the colour from the Custom colors list.

5 The colour's details appear here

6 Click the Add to Custom Colors button to create a custom colour

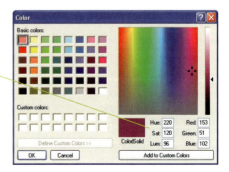

Optimising images

The combination of good quality images and small file sizes is known as optimisation. This is an important aspect of using images on the Internet as the file sizes have to be as small as possible to speed up downloading time while still retaining a suitable image quality. This chapter explains the basics behind optimising images and shows the ways in which it can be achieved in Fireworks.

Covers

Why optimise images? | 66

Previewing images | 67

Optimize panel | 68

Applying optimisation | 69

Export Preview | 70

Export Wizard | 71

Quick Export | 73

Transparency | 75

Chapter Five

Why optimise images?

The issue of optimising images is essentially one that concerns images that are going to be used on the Internet, either as part of a Web page or as an email attachment. What optimising is concerned with is creating the best quality image, with the smallest file size. The issue of file size is paramount because this effects the way it is downloaded over the Internet: the bigger the file size, the longer it takes to download. As Internet users become more sophisticated, so the issue of downloading time takes centre stage: if people are not prepared to wait for your images to download, they will quickly move on to something else.

If images on the Internet have been optimised effectively, it is sometimes hard to tell any difference in quality between one of a large file size and a much smaller one.

As far as optimising images is concerned, viewing them on computers has one big advantage: a computer monitor can only display a certain amount of colour (usually 72–96 pixels, or coloured dots, for every inch of monitor space). This means that a lot of colour information can be discarded without any noticeable loss of quality on a monitor. There is an entire industry devoted to the issue of optimising images for use on the Internet and it has come up with some dramatic developments over the years.

The Fireworks proprietary image format, PNG (Portable Network Graphic), can also be used on the Internet, but it has not been as widely accepted as GIFs and JPEGs.

GIFs or JPEGs

The two main image formats used on the Internet are GIFs (Graphical Interchange Format) and JPEGs (Joint Photographic Experts Group). Both use systems of image compression to ensure that the images are as compact as possible. JPEGs use up to 16 million colours and are best for displaying photographic images, while GIFs only use 256 colours and are better suited for continuous tone images. However, both formats can be used for all types of images and there is not as big a difference between 256 and 16 million as you might think.

When using images on Web pages, try and keep them below 50 KB in size, if possible.

With terms like compression and image resolution being frequently used in relation to optimising images, it can seem like a complicated business and, behind the scenes, it is. However, Fireworks provides step-by-step guidance to make the process as simple as possible.

Previewing images

In the work area it is possible to preview the download time of the image you are currently working on. This will give you an idea of whether you need to optimise it or not.

1 Click here to preview the current image. This is how it will appear when published on a Web page

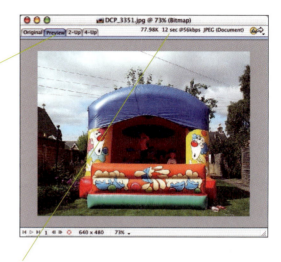

In the Preview panel, the downloading time is estimated using a modem that downloads at 28 kbps. Obviously, if a quicker modem is being used, or cable, the downloading time will be faster.

2 The image size, downloading time and image type are shown here

Images can also be previewed with two or four options on screen:

Click here to preview two versions of the image

Click here to preview four versions of the image

When the 2-Up or 4-Up preview options are selected, all of the images retain the attributes of the original. However, it is possible to use these panels to optimise the image and view the different results.

Optimize panel

The main tool for optimising images is the Optimize panel. This displays the attributes for the currently selected image. The Optimize panel works with several image formats but the most common for use on the Web are GIF and JPEG formats. To use the Optimize panel:

1 Select Window>Optimize from the Menu bar

2 Click here to select GIF or JPEG settings

There are various colour palettes that can be used within the GIF settings. Most of these ensure that all colours used are, or are converted to, Web-safe colours i.e. ones that will appear the same on all Web browsers.

3 Select settings for the selected image type in the Optimize panel

Dithering is an option in the GIF optimize panel and is a technique that is used to compensate for the fact that GIFs only use 256 colours.

4 Click here to give a preset name to a group of settings that have been selected. This will then appear in the Settings box

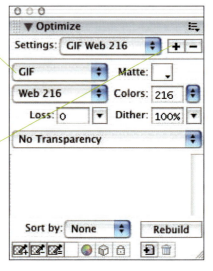

Applying optimisation

To optimise an image and then save it:

 Select either the Preview, 2-Up or 4-Up panel

 Click on one of the image windows

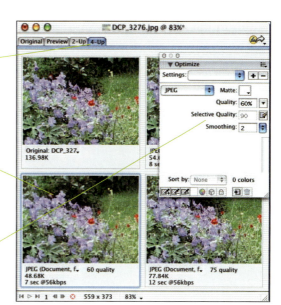

 Apply settings from the Optimize panel

 When you have the best optimise settings, select File>Export from the Menu bar and save the image to your hard drive

 Once the image has been exported and saved check in the file's directory to make sure it has been saved as the correct type of file

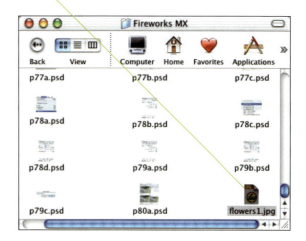

Export Preview

If you want to get a clearer look at the way an image will appear with a certain set of optimise settings, you can do so with the Export Preview function:

1 Select an image and apply optimisation settings

2 Select File>Export Preview from the Menu bar

3 The Export Preview window is an enlarged version of the image preview windows, and it also includes the settings from the Optimize panel. These can be edited before exporting

4 Click Export to save the image with the current settings

Export Wizard

For anyone who does not feel completely confident about optimising and exporting images, there is a wizard that guides you through all of the required steps. To use the Export Wizard:

If you select File>Export in Original mode, without the use of Export Preview, Export Wizard or the Optimize panel, the image will be exported in the same format as it was opened in. So if it was opened as a GIF, this is the format in which it will be exported. If you want to export it to another format then the optimise settings have to be changed in either the Optimize panel or during the export process with Export Preview or Export Wizard.

1 Select the image you want to export, from either the Original, Preview, 2-Up or 4-Up panels

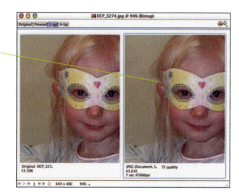

2 Select File>Export Wizard from the Menu bar

3 Click here to enable the Wizard to select an appropriate file format.

If you want an image to be optimised to a certain size, click here and enter the target size that you want the image to be. The Wizard will automatically set the image's attributes to meet this file size.

4 Click Continue

By default, the settings chosen by the Export Wizard for images to be used on the Web or with Dreamweaver are GIF or JPEG format. For image editing and desktop publishing applications, the default format is TIFF.

5 Specify how you intend to use the image. The Wizard will then select the most appropriate file format. Click Continue

6 A dialog box will detail the selected file format and explain any issues connected with it. Click Exit to continue

If you want to export an image with a transparent background, it has to be in a GIF format. For more on creating transparent images, see pages 75–76.

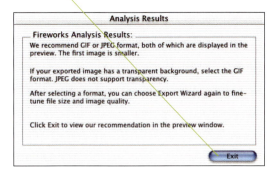

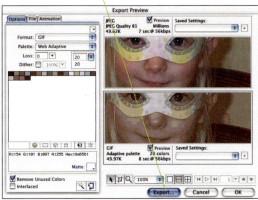

The Export Preview window displays an alternative format option for the selected image, if it has been accessed through the Export Wizard.

7 The Export Preview dialog will appear. This is the same as on page 70. Edit any settings as required and Click Export to export and save the file

Quick Export

The Quick Export function enables Fireworks documents to be exported into file formats other than image ones. These include HTML files, Flash files and also plain HTML code. To use Quick Export:

1   Open an image

2   Click here to access the Quick Export options

The Export options appear after the required export format has been selected. Each format has its own menu of Export options.

3   Select the required export format

4   Select the Export options for the selected format

5   Select a location for the file and click on Save

The selected file format is displayed in the Export dialog box.

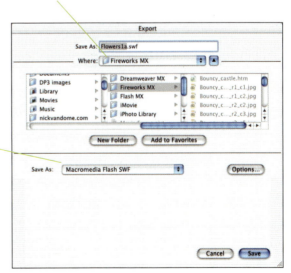

Exporting HTML code

If you are creating Web pages, it can be useful to copying the HTML code from a Fireworks document (such as a rollover or a sliced image) so that it can then be pasted into a HTML document. To do this:

1 Select Copy HTML Code from the Quick Export menu

2 Select the required HTML style and click Next

Once HTML code has been saved it can then be opened and copied and pasted into any Web authoring program. However, since Dreamweaver works so closely with Fireworks, this is the best option to use. There are various options in Dreamweaver for inserting HTML code into documents.

3 Enter a name for any slices (i.e. if the image has been broken up into different parts) used in the document and click Next

4 Browse for a location in which to save the HTML code and click Finish

Transparency

One of the most effective techniques for displaying images on Web pages is to make their background transparent, to enable Web backgrounds to be visible behind the main element in an image.

Index transparency

This is used to make specific colours transparent:

Only images in GIF or PNG 8 format can have transparency applied to them for use on Web pages.

Alpha transparency can also be used in a similar way to index transparency, but this is not usually used for Web graphics as most browsers do not support this format.

1 Open an image and select GIF or PNG 8 as the file format in the Optimize panel

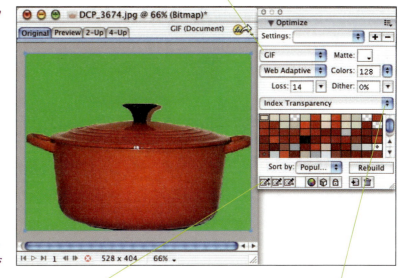

3 Click here to add a colour to the Index Transparency list

2 Click here and select Index Transparency

4 Click on the image. The colour at this point will then become transparent wherever it occurs in the image

When applying transparency, the effect can only be seen in Preview, 2-Up or 4-Up mode. It cannot be seen if the image is being viewed in Original mode.

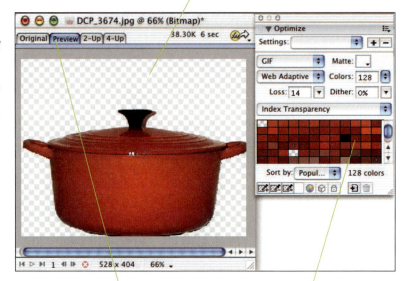

5 Click on the Preview tab to view the transparent effect

6 Click here to make other colours used in the image transparent

One of the best uses of transparency is for an item where you want to make the whole background transparent, such as with a company logo. This means that the image will blend into a Web page background rather than appear to sit on top of it.

7 When viewed as a Web page, the background of the page shows through behind the image

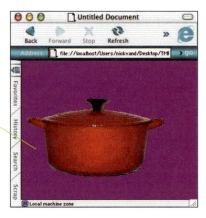

Web authoring with Fireworks

Fireworks is closely integrated with the Web authoring program, Dreamweaver. This chapter shows how the two programs can be used together to speed up workflow when working with images and Web pages. It also gives an overview of creating entire Web pages in Fireworks.

Covers

Fireworks and Dreamweaver | 78

Roundtrip image editing | 79

Resizing images | 81

Creating Web pages in Fireworks | 83

Chapter Six

Fireworks and Dreamweaver

Since images are an integral part of websites, it makes sense for companies to closely integrate their Web authoring tools with their image editing ones. That is exactly what Macromedia have done with Fireworks and Dreamweaver. Dreamweaver is the Macromedia Web authoring program and it is widely regarded as one of the best tools for the job on the market, particularly by professional designers. It has a powerful array of features to satisfy even the most demanding of designers and it has an interface that can enable people to get up and running with the program quickly.

For a detailed view of Dreamweaver, take a look at 'Dreamweaver MX in easy steps'.

With the latest versions of Fireworks and Dreamweaver it is possible to move seamlessly between the two to edit images and create elements for Web pages. In addition, the user interfaces are designed in the same way, so when you move from one to another you will still be in a familiar working environment. Some of the functions that can be performed with Fireworks and Dreamweaver are:

For more information about slices and hotspots, see Chapter Seven. For more information on rollovers and pop-up menus, see Chapter Nine.

- Roundtrip image editing. This means you can open a page in Dreamweaver and then edit images directly in Fireworks: you do not have to open the image separately, edit it and then place it back into Dreamweaver. When you have finished editing the image in Fireworks, the changes are automatically applied to the Dreamweaver document

- Importing HTML files used to create more complex items such as slices, hotspots, rollovers and pop-up menus. Since Fireworks is not just an image editor it can also create HTML documents. The designer specifies which images to use in a document and the functions they are going to perform, e.g. two different images that are going to be combined as a rollover button, and then Fireworks creates all of the necessary files and code to create the effect. It is then a case of importing the images and HTML into Dreamweaver. This gives designers a great deal of power and flexibility

If you are going to be using a Web authoring program then it should definitely be Dreamweaver if you use Fireworks.

Roundtrip image editing

Before images are added to a page in Dreamweaver they will probably already have been edited and optimised in Fireworks. However, if further work is required, this can be done by accessing Fireworks directly from Dreamweaver. To do this:

A contextual menu is one that contains options that apply to the currently selected item. These are always accessed by right-clicking (Windows) or Ctrl+click (Mac) on an item on the page.

1 Right-click (Windows) or Ctrl+click (Mac) the image you want to edit in Dreamweaver

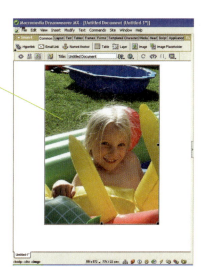

You can also select Optimize in Fireworks from the contextual menu, in which case you will be taken to a dialog box in Fireworks which is the same as the Export Preview one.

2 Select Edit with Fireworks from the contextual menu

3 In the Find Source dialog box, select No, unless you want to edit an existing PNG file

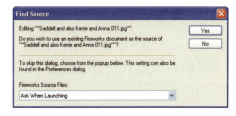

Roundtrip editing can also be accessed by selecting an image in Dreamweaver and clicking on the Edit button on the Properties Inspector.

4 The image is opened in the normal Fireworks environment, except that it indicates here that the document is one that is being edited from Dreamweaver

If you select File>Update while editing the image in Fireworks, the changes will be applied within the Dreamweaver document but you will remain in Fireworks. To apply the changes and return to Dreamweaver, the Done button has to be selected.

5 Apply editing changes as you normally would within Fireworks (in this case parts of the image have been recoloured)

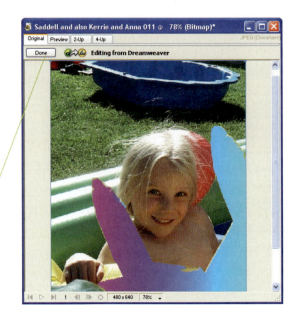

If you have edited the size of an image in Fireworks, you will need to reset the size when you return to Dreamweaver. See the next two pages for details on how to do this.

6 Click Done

7 You will be taken back to Dreamweaver and the original image will have had the editing changes applied to it

Once an image has been updated with roundtrip editing, the original will also have been changed, not just the version in Dreamweaver. Make sure that any editing changes you make are ones you want to apply permanently before selecting Done in Fireworks.

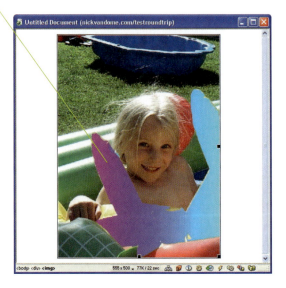

Resizing images

It is possible to resize images in a Dreamweaver document by applying the changes in a similar way to the editing changes shown on the previous two pages. However, there is one extra step that also needs to be applied:

It is possible to resize an image within the Dreamweaver environment by selecting it and dragging the resizing handles. However this results in poorer image quality than if it is resized in Fireworks.

1 Right-click (Windows) or Ctrl+click (Mac) on an image in a Dreamweaver document and select Edit in Fireworks from the contextual menu

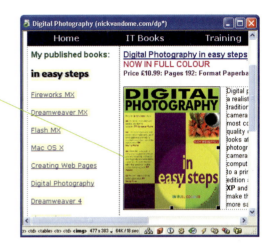

2 In Fireworks, select Modify>Canvas>Image Size from the Menu bar

When entering values for editing the image size, check the Constrain Proportions box to ensure that the image is resized proportionally, i.e. when the height value is changed the width value is updated automatically to keep the image in the correct proportion, and vice versa.

3 Enter the new image size values here

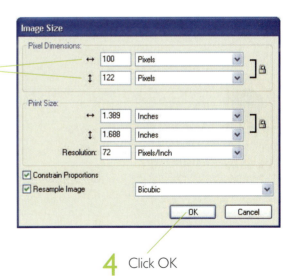

4 Click OK

If other image editing changes have been applied to an image, these will appear when the image is viewed again in Dreamweaver. However, any resizing changes have to be applied by using the Reset command.

5 In Dreamweaver, the image initially appears the same size as originally

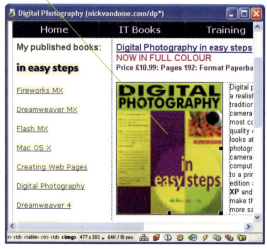

The Reset Size function can also be applied by selecting an image and clicking on the Reset button on the Properties Inspector in Dreamweaver.

6 Right-click (Windows) or Ctrl+click (Mac) on the image and select Reset Size from the contextual menu

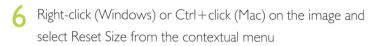

7 The image size that was specified in Fireworks is now applied to the image in Dreamweaver

Do not change the size of an image too many times. If this is done then the quality of the image will deteriorate noticeably.

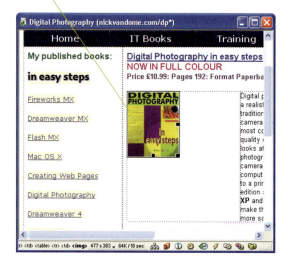

Creating Web pages in Fireworks

In addition to creating and manipulating images, Fireworks can also be used to create entire websites. This is done by adding all of the necessary elements and then exporting them as one HTML file and all of the image files that make up the finished page. Backgrounds, images, text, buttons and rollovers can all be included in this way. To create a Web page in Fireworks:

Since Web pages created in Fireworks are image based, i.e. all of the content is made up of images, there can be some accessibility issues. This concerns people who are blind or partially sighted and who access websites with software that reads the content on screen. This can be difficult if all of the content is made up of images.

1 Add a background colour

2 Add objects with coloured or gradient fills

3 Add text

4 Import images

Not all website designs should be as bright as the example on this page. In a lot of cases a subtle, understated, design is the most effective. However, for some sites, such as those for children, colourful sites are a definite option.

5 Add buttons to create a navigation bar

6 Add slices or hotspots over any elements of the page, as required

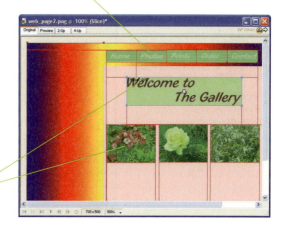

7 Export the Fireworks document as shown in Chapter 7 page 96

8 The files can then be published or imported into Dreamweaver to be edited further. To do this, select Fireworks HTML in Dreamweaver and select the HTML file. Click Open

When the Fireworks document is exported, one HTML file is created and all of the elements of the page are broken up into individual images, or sliced images. For more information on creating slices, see Chapter Seven.

9 The page can then be edited in Dreamweaver, if required, and published on the Web

When uploading a website created in Fireworks, all of the sliced image files must be uploaded as well as the HTML file. Otherwise some parts of the page will not be displayed properly.

Slices, hotspots and layers

Slices and hotspots can be used to create HTML code that can give images increased functionality. This chapter gives an overview of slices and hotspots and shows some of the uses to which they can be put. It also shows how layers and masks can be used to combine graphics together into a single image.

Covers

About slices | 86

Creating slices | 87

Slice options | 89

Optimising slices | 90

Text slices | 91

Reconstituting tables | 92

Creating hotspots | 95

Exporting slices and hotspots | 96

Creating layers | 97

Web layer | 98

Working with layers | 99

Blending | 102

Creating masks | 103

Editing masks | 104

Chapter Seven

About slices

Although slices take on a physical appearance within Fireworks, they are in fact HTML code that adds certain elements of functionality to images. Slices can be edited within a Fireworks document, and then the whole file can be exported for use within a Web page. Slices are used to cut up images into smaller parts and then various functions can be applied. The main uses for slices are:

Cutting up large images

When you see an image on a website that is being downloaded a segment at a time, this is probably because it has been created using slicing.

Large images take longer to download on a Web page than a lot of small ones. With slices, it is possible to cut an image up into several smaller parts. Once it is exported and viewed as a Web page, the different parts are reassembled to display the entire image again. Since this uses a lot of smaller images, this results in faster downloading times. In addition, it is possible to optimise different parts of a sliced image. So if one area of the image does not have to be as prominent as another, this can be optimised to create a smaller file size.

Creating interactivity

For more information about creating rollover buttons, navigation bars and rollovers, see Chapter Nine.

Slices can be used to apply interactivity to certain areas of an image. For instance, a slice could be created for buttons, pop-up menus or rollover items. This is done by instructing the slice to display another item when the cursor is passed over it. In this way slices can be a very powerful tool for use on a Web page.

Swapping images

Sliced elements of an image are created as individual image files. These can then be edited independently of each other if required.

If there are a number of different elements within an image, slices can be used to update one image, without having to edit the whole thing. For instance, if there is an image that displays a weekly special offer on an e-commerce site, slicing could be used to update the special offer item without having to touch the rest of the image. In this respect a sliced image can be thought of as a jigsaw puzzle: it is cut up in Fireworks and then the pieces are put together within a browser. If you need to replace one piece, this can be done without disturbing anything else.

Creating slices

There are three ways to create slices in Fireworks:

Menu bar option

When a slice is created, Fireworks generates a table structure in which the slice resides. This is denoted by lines around the object that is being sliced.

1 Select an object with the Pointer tool, or part of an object with the Marquee tool

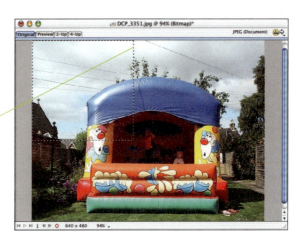

Slices created in this way are always done so as rectangle. So if you insert a slice over an oval or a circle, it will cover a larger area than the object itself.

2 Select Edit>Insert>Slice from the Menu bar

3 The slice is inserted over the object and appears by default as a transparent green rectangle

When a slice is created, the name of the file format of the image that is being sliced is displayed on top of the slice.

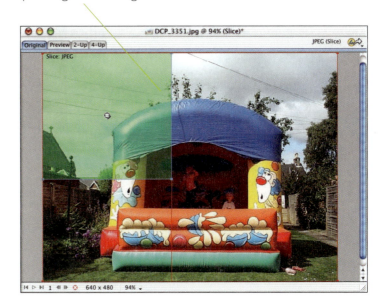

Slice tool option

1 Select the Slice tool from the Tools panel

When creating multiple slices on an object, be careful not to overlap them. This could effect the way they are viewed in a browser or any interactivity that is applied to them.

2 Click and drag on an image to create a slice

Polygon Slice tool option

To access the Polygon Slice tool, click on the black triangle next to the Slice tool on the Tools panel.

1 Select the Polygon Slice tool from the Tools panel

When using the Polygon Slice tool, click back at the starting point to finish creating the polygon shape.

2 Click at the point where you want to begin the slice

3 Click at each point where you want to create a change of direction. Create an irregular slice object in this way

Slice options

Once a slice has been created it can be edited and manipulated with the Properties Inspector and the Tools panel:

Properties Inspector

The Properties Inspector can be used to add a URL (hyperlink) to a slice and specify its name and colour:

Enter alternative text   Enter a URL   Enter a target location (if required)

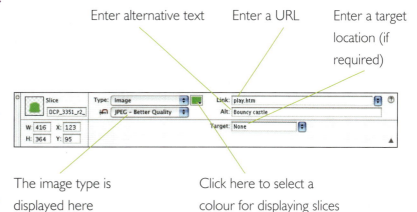

The image type is displayed here

Click here to select a colour for displaying slices

Tools panel

The Tools panel can be used to hide slices so that the images underneath them can be edited. To do this:

Click here on the Tools panel to hide all slices (and hotspots)

Click here on the Tools panel to show all slices (and hotspots)

Optimising slices

Slices can be optimised in the same way as optimising whole images. However, it is possible to apply different levels of optimisation to different slices:

When slices are exported the sliced area becomes an image in its own right, with code inserted into an HTML document that instructs a browser how to reconstruct the whole sliced image.

1   Select an image that contains two or more slices. Select one of the slices by clicking on it once with the Pointer tool

Slices on a single image can be optimised in different file formats i.e. you can mix GIFs and JPEGs. When the image is reassembled in a browser, the different file formats will appear together.

2   Apply optimisation attributes in the Optimize panel

3   Select another slice

4   Apply different optimisation settings to this slice

Text slices

Slices can also be used to create text on images. This is done by converting text into an image file. It is then possible to update the text without affecting the rest of the image. To create a text slice:

1 Insert a slice on an image

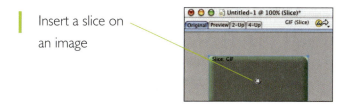

2 Select HTML here on the Properties Inspector

3 Click here to edit the slice

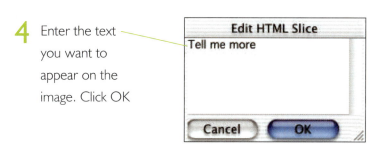

4 Enter the text you want to appear on the image. Click OK

5 Select File>Export from the Menu bar and select Save in the Export dialog box

6 When the image is viewed in a browser, the text is a slice but appears normally

Reconstituting tables

If you are creating Web pages within a team it is not uncommon for files to get lost or deleted by mistake. Sometimes this means that the source files have to be recreated, which can be a time-consuming business, particularly if the source files contained complex formatting such as rollovers and sliced images. However, in Fireworks MX there is a function whereby tables created with slices and hotspots can be reconstituted so that the source images are restored. They can then be edited individually rather than having to recreate everything from scratch. To reconstitute tables:

Slices and hotspots are always created in a table format. This is then used to create the HTML code for displaying the slices or hotspots on a Web page.

1 Select File>Reconstitute Table from the Menu bar (a file does not have to be open at this point)

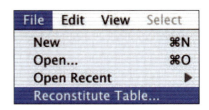

2 Select a HTML file from which you want to reconstitute the elements within it

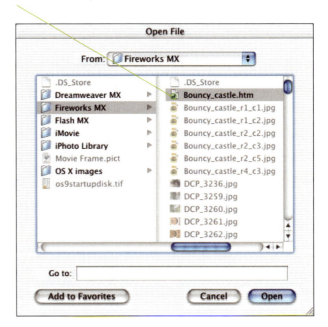

3 Click Open

4 The file opens with the table and image displayed

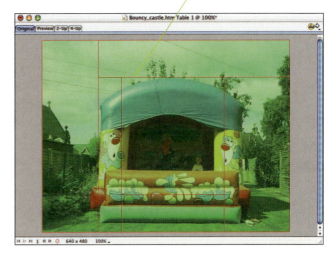

A HTML document must consist of at least one table in order for Fireworks to reconstitute it.

5 Select File>Save (or Save As) from the Menu bar

6 The file is saved as a PNG file (the proprietary Fireworks format)

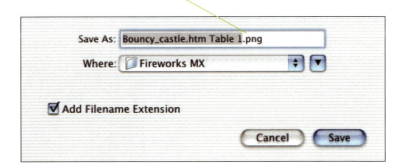

7 Click Save

8 The source PNG file can then be opened in the normal way

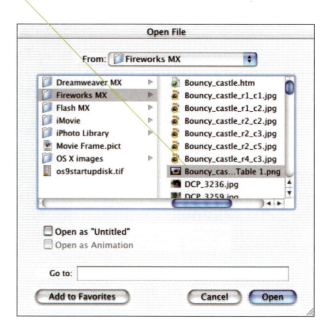

9 The source file can then be edited. This is particularly useful if text has been added to an image)

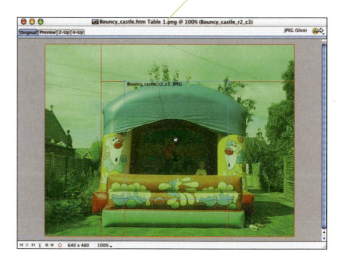

Creating hotspots

Hotspots can be used to create hyperlinks to different addresses, from within the same image. This end result is known as an image map and it can be used as a useful navigation device on a Web page. For instance, it could be used on a physical map to link to pages containing information about a particular country, or an e-commerce site could contain an image with hotspots over each product. When the user clicks on that product the hotspot takes them to details about that item. To create hotspots:

Hotspots and image maps are also an effective way to create navigation bars. To do this, create the design for the navigation bar and then create an image map by drawing hotspots over each area that will navigate to another part of the site.

1 Select the Rectangle or Circle Hotspot tool from the Tools panel

The third hotspot option is the Polygon Hotspot tool. This is used to create irregular hotspots as opposed to symmetrical ones. These can be created in the same way as creating irregular slices (see page 88).

2 Draw hotspots on the image as required

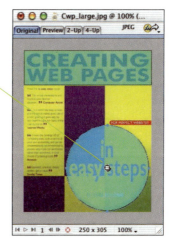

3 Select each hotspot and, in the Properties Inspector, enter a URL, alternative text and a target location (if required)

Exporting slices and hotspots

Once images have had slices or hotspots added to them, they can be exported so that they can be used on Web pages. To do this:

1 Add slices or hotspots to an image and select File>Export from the Menu bar

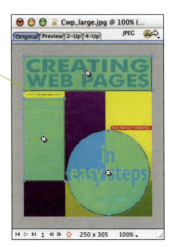

If you select Copy to Clipboard as the HTML option, the code can then be pasted into a HTML authoring program such as Dreamweaver. This is the same process as performed by the Quick Export>Copy HTML Code function.

2 Select the location where you want the files to be saved. Select HTML and Images

3 Select Export HTML File

4 Select Export Slices

5 Click Save

Creating layers

Layers are used in Fireworks to place items on different levels within the same image. It is similar to drawing objects on several pieces of transparent film and then combining them to create the overall image. By using layers, images can be edited independently of one another and they can greatly simplify things when working with complex images. In addition, blending and masking techniques can be used to merge images together. Working with layers is done with the Layers panel. To access the Layers panel and create layers:

The top layer in the Layers panel is always the Web layer. This contains Web objects such as hotspots and slices, and they always reside on this layer, regardless of how many Web objects there are. For more on this, see the next page.

1   Select Window>Layers from the Menu bar

2   The active layer is denoted by the pencil icon

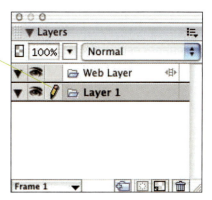

It is particularly important to use layers if you are working with complex images with numerous different elements.

3   Add content to the work area. This is shown underneath the active layer

Web layer

The top layer in the Layers panel is always the Web layer, which contains Web objects such as hotspots, slices and rollovers. Even if these items are inserted when another layer is selected they will automatically be placed in the Web layer. To use the Web layer:

The Web layer cannot be deleted or renamed, although the items within it can be.

1 With the Layers panel showing, insert a hotspot or a slice in the work area

Objects in the Web layer are visible across all frames within an image.

2 The Web object appears under the Web layer

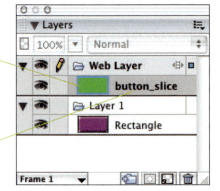

3 Double-click on the Web object and type a new name

4 Select a Web object and click on the wastebasket icon to remove it from the Web layer and also the active document

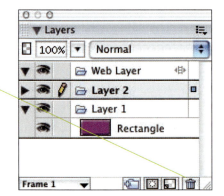

Working with layers

Using the Layers panel, it is possible to edit and manipulate layers in a number of ways:

Adding layers

1 Click here to add a new layer

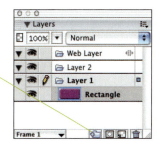

Items on layers at the top of the stacking order i.e. those nearest to the Web layer, can overlap the images on the layers below them, if they are positioned on top of them.

2 Add content to the new layer. Although this can overlap items on other layers it does not interact with them

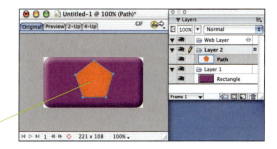

Naming layers

1 Double-click on the layer name

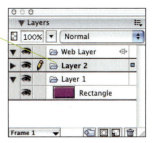

2 Enter a new name for the layer and press Enter or Return

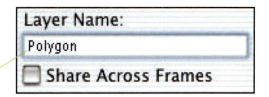

Selecting layers or items on layers

Click on a layer
or an item in the
Layers panel

or

Click on an item in
the work area

*If you are
trying to edit a
particular item
and the
changes are not
taking effect, make sure that
the correct layer is selected.*

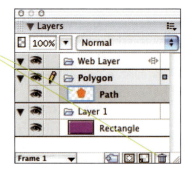

Deleting layers or items on layers

Select a layer or
an item on a layer
and click on the
wastebasket icon

Hiding layers

*When a layer is
made invisible,
the items on it
are still in
place, they are
just hidden from
view.*

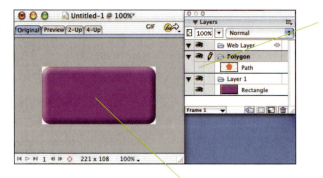

Click here
so that the
eye icon
disappears

2 The items on the selected layer are no longer visible

Locking layers

When a layer has been locked, it cannot be selected and the items on it cannot be edited. This is a useful option if you want to ensure you do not change any items on a layer by mistake. To unlock a layer, click the padlock icon.

Click here to display a padlock icon

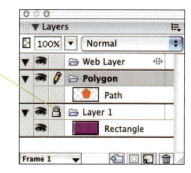

Setting transparency

| Select an item in the work area

Different items within a single layer can have separate opacity settings applied to them.

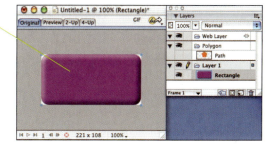

2 Click here and drag the slider to set the level of opacity

Select Modify> Flatten Layers to merge all of the layers in an image into a single layer.

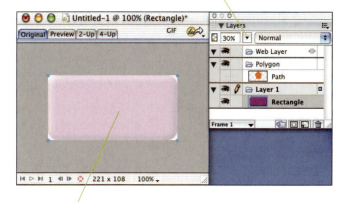

3 The item on the layer will display the new opacity setting

Blending

Blending can be used to create artistic effects by combining the colours of different objects. Blending can be used between objects on the same layer or different layers. To use blending:

1 Select an object that overlaps another, either on the same layer or a different one

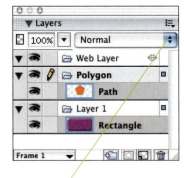

2 Click here to select a blend effect

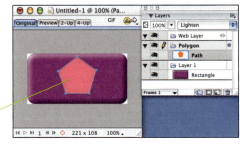

3 The effect is applied to the selected item in the work area. In this case the effect is Lighten

Creating masks

Masks can be created to cover existing objects and determine the area that is visible. When a mask is placed over an object, only the area covered by the mask is visible. To create a mask:

1 Create an object which is going to be masked, or import a bitmap image

Text can also be used as a mask. To do this, create the text using the Text tool and then cut it and paste it as a mask.

2 Create the mask object, in vector mode, with the drawing tools

3 Select the mask object and select Edit>Cut from the Menu bar

The Marquee tools can also be used to create masks. To do this, make a selection with a Marquee tool, then select Modify>Mask>Reveal Selection from the Menu bar.

4 Select the original object and select Edit>Paste as Mask from the Menu bar

5 The original object is now only visible through the mask

Editing masks

When masks are applied to an image or graphic, the two objects become linked. However, it is still possible to edit them separately:

1 Click here to remove the link between the mask and the graphic

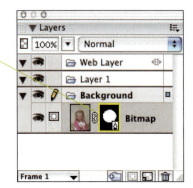

If the mask and the graphic are linked, they can be moved as one item. This is shown by them both moving in the thumbnails in the Layers panel.

2 Click here to select the mask

or

Click here to select the graphic

To remove a mask, select it in the Layers panel and select Modify>Mask>Delete Mask from the Menu bar. Then select Discard in the dialog box that appears.

3 Click and drag to move the location of the mask or the graphic

Masks can be scaled, rotated, skewed or distorted in the same way as any other object.

Buttons and navigation bars

Buttons and navigation bars are two of the most popular devices for providing navigation around websites. These are images that have interactivity added to them so that they can change appearance and also take the user to other Web pages. This chapter shows the processes for creating buttons and navigation bars.

Covers

About buttons | 106

Creating buttons | 107

Buttons and the Library | 111

Editing buttons | 113

Exporting buttons | 114

Navigation bars | 115

Chapter Eight

About buttons

Buttons can be used as the basis for creating navigation bars. For more information on this, see pages 115–116.

Buttons are a common device used on Web pages to give them a more pleasing design aspect. They are created using Javascript code and they change appearance according to whether they are untouched, the cursor is moved over them or they are in the process of being pressed. Most commonly, buttons have two states: a static one (Up) and one when the cursor moves over them (Over). In Fireworks it is possible to create designs for the way buttons will look and then all of the complicated Javascript code is inserted automatically.

Up state of a button   Over state of a button

For more information on symbols and instances see Chapter Ten.

Symbols

Buttons that are created in Fireworks are a type of symbol, which means they can be stored in the Library and instances can be inserted into documents. An instance is a reference back to a symbol and, as such, it does not occupy a physical presence itself. If the original symbol is altered, then all instances that are based on it are changed too.

Buttons in Fireworks are a very flexible device, which can be quickly edited using the Button Editor. They can also have text added to all elements of the button in one operation, there is no need to go into each state separately to update it.

Symbols and instances help to keep the sizes of files and images as small as possible, which decreases downloading time when viewed on the Web.

If you want to give your Web pages an added touch of class then creating buttons in Fireworks is an excellent way to start.

Creating buttons

Buttons are created in the Button Editor, which is similar to the normal Fireworks work area, except that it contains panels for creating the different states of a button. The content for the button can be added in the same way as when creating objects in the normal work area. The Button Editor can only be accessed when a document has already been opened. When the button has been created it will appear within the original document. To create a button:

The Button Editor can be used to insert buttons into images that already contain content. This is generally done if you are creating more complex elements for Web pages, rather than just straightforward buttons.

1   Open a new document and select Edit>Insert>New Button from the Menu bar

2   The Button Editor opens in the Up state panel

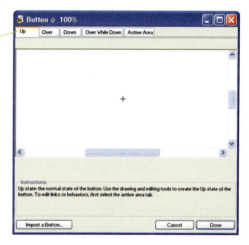

3   Enter content for the Up state of the button. This can be an object with a fill, style and stroke

The most common technique when designing the Up and Over states of a button is to keep the text style the same and just change the text colour and the fill colour of the button. This achieves an effective transition from one state of the button to another.

4 Click on the Over tab. Click on the Copy Up Graphic button if you want this state of the button to be similar to the Up state

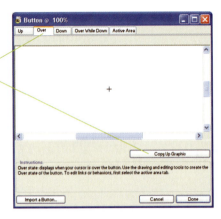

5 Edit the button for the Over state

The content for the Down and Over While Down states can be copied from the previous states in the same way as the Over state is copied from the Up state.

6 If required, add content for the Down and Over While Down States

7 Click on the Active Area tab. This is the area that the user will click on to activate the button

Although the Active Area will appear to contain content, this is just to show the area that it covers. The fill and stroke can be anything, as it does not appear in the finished button.

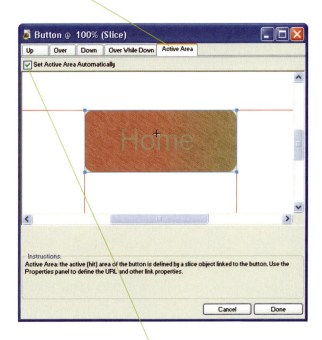

The active area of a button should generally be the same size as the button itself. If not, it could cause confusion when the button is viewed on a browser.

8 Click here to set the Active Area automatically

9 In the Properties Inspector enter a hyperlink here

When adding a link, add Alt text too. This is the text that will appear when the cursor is moved over the button or if a browser has been set to not display images.

10 Click Done to close the Button Editor

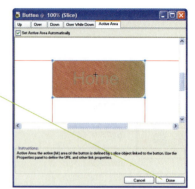

When a button is created, it is automatically placed in the Library as a symbol. This can then be placed into documents directly from the Library.

11 Select Modify>Canvas>Trim Canvas from the Menu bar to make the canvas the same size as the button

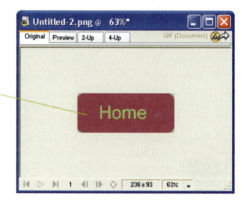

If the canvas is not trimmed to size, there may be unwanted space around the button when it is exported and then viewed on a browser. Make sure that only the button is visible.

12 To add a link to a button once it has been created, enter it here in the URL panel, or in the Properties Inspector

Buttons and the Library

Once a button has been created, it becomes a symbol and is automatically placed in the Library. Instances of the button can then be used in the active document. Once an instance has been inserted, its attributes can be modified in the Properties Inspector. This means that different instances of a button symbol can have different text and different hyperlinks applied to them. To use button symbols from the Library:

If you want to change the graphical appearance of a button, this has to be done by editing the button (see page 113).

1   Select a button symbol in the Library and drag it into an active document to make an instance of it

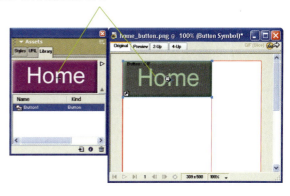

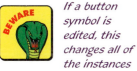

If a button symbol is edited, this changes all of the instances of that button.

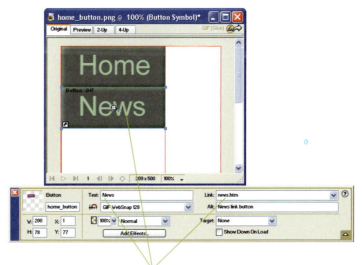

2   Select a button instance and alter its text and hyperlink attributes in the Properties Inspector

Using existing buttons

Fireworks MX has a preset Library of buttons that have already been created. This can be used to insert buttons into existing documents. To use the buttons Library:

1 Select Edit>Libraries>Buttons from the Menu bar

2 Select a button type and click here to preview its different states

There are other library collections that can be accessed by selecting Edit>Libraries from the Menu bar. The available collections include Animations, Bullets and Themes.

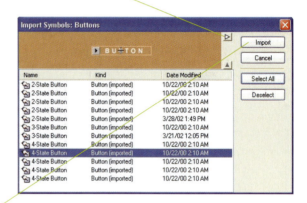

3 Click here to import the button into the existing document's Library

4 The button symbol is placed in the Library and can be used in the same way as any other button symbol

Editing buttons

All states of a button can be edited at any point before the button is exported. Fill, stroke and text can all be edited in the Button Editor.

Button Editor

Text can be edited in the Button Editor by clicking on the existing text with the Text tool.

1 Double-click the button in the work area or in the top panel of the Library

2 Edit the fill, stroke or text of one or all of the states of the button

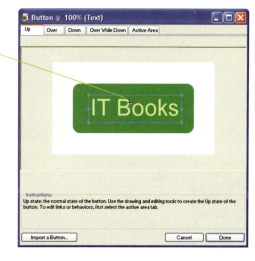

Click on Import a Button in the Button Editor to import a button from the Button Library, as shown on the previous page.

3 Click Done

4 Select Yes to update the text in the other button states

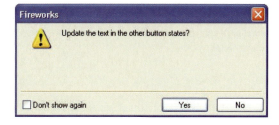

Exporting buttons

Once buttons have been created, they have to be exported so that the necessary code can be created for them to be able to function on a Web page. When a button is exported, image files are created for the different states and a HTML file is created for the code. To export a button:

Before a button is exported, select the Preview, 2-Up or 4-Up panels, to see how the button will function when it is active i.e. viewed in a browser. Rollover the button and click it to preview its different states.

1 Select File > Export from the Menu bar

2 Enter a name for the button

3 Select HTML and Images

4 Select Export HTML file

5 Select Export Slices

Once a button has been exported it can be inserted into a Dreamweaver document by using the Insert Fireworks HTML command on the Common tab of the Insert panel and then selecting the HTML file that is created during the export process.

6 Click Save

7 View your file structure to check that the HTML and image files have been created

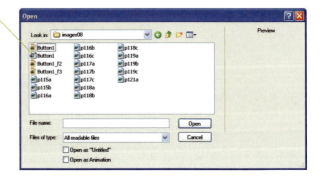

Navigation bars

A navigation bar is a collection of buttons that are displayed horizontally or vertically on a Web page. Ideally, it should also appear on all of the pages within a specific website. This means there is a consistency on all pages and users will feel comfortable when they are navigating around the site. To create a navigation bar:

Always include a link back to a site's Home Page on a navigation bar. This way, users will have a quick way to get back to the point where they started and, if the navigation bar is on all the pages of the site, they will not feel as if they are lost within the site.

1 Create a button symbol that will be the basis of the navigation bar

When duplicating buttons, it may be necessary to increase the canvas size by selecting Modify>Canvas>Canvas Size from the Menu bar.

2 Insert the necessary number of instances into the active document by dragging them from the Library

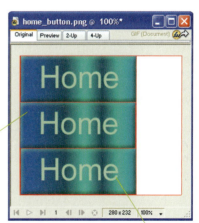

3 Position the button instances either horizontally or vertically to create the navigation bar

The links on the buttons of a navigation bar can be edited within the HTML code in a Web authoring program such as Dreamweaver.

The design of buttons can be as simple or as complex as you like for use in navigation bars. However, make sure they all have the same appearance. The only items that should change from button to button are the button text and the link.

4 Select each button and enter its unique text and hyperlink attributes in the Properties Inspector

5 Select Modify > Canvas > Trim Canvas from the Menu bar to ensure the navigation bar does not take up any unnecessary space

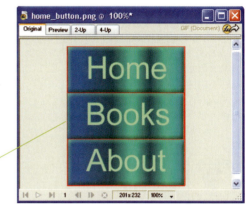

6 Select File > Export from the Menu bar and select the same options as for exporting a single button (see page 114)

7 When the navigation bar is imported into a Web authoring program such as Dreamweaver it appears as a single image. However, when it is previewed in a browser, each button on the navigation bar operates independently of the others

Rollovers

Rollovers can be used to create some of the most eye-catching and effective elements on a Web page. This chapter shows how to create rollovers using different techniques. It also details how to create simple rollovers, disjoint rollovers and pop-up menus.

Covers

About rollovers | 118

Creating rollovers with behaviors | 119

Drag-and-drop rollovers | 122

Creating disjoint rollovers | 124

Creating pop-up menus | 127

Editing pop-up menus | 134

Combining slices and hotspots | 135

Editing behaviors | 138

Exporting rollovers | 140

Chapter Nine

About rollovers

Rollovers are a frequently used device on Web pages. They are created with Javascript and can be used to create different types of effects when a cursor interacts with them on a Web page. A button, such as those shown in the previous chapter, is a simple example of a rollover: when the cursor rolls over the initial image, this is replaced with another one. However rollovers can be used to create complex and effective design features:

Rollovers are created using slices and frames. Different images are accommodated in different frames and the slices are used to connect the two and apply the required effect.

Swap one image with another when the cursor rolls over the initial image

The two elements of a disjoint rollover should be kept within reasonable proximity of each other. Otherwise it may not be clear that they are connected.

Create a disjoint rollover, where an image or text appears at a different point from the initial image

Pop-up menus are very useful if you have a lot of sub-headings, or topics, that you want to link to one main heading or topic. The user can then navigate to the sub-heading without having to leave the main menu.

Create a pop-up menu for enhanced navigation

Creating rollovers with behaviors

Rollovers can be created by using the following elements:

- A trigger Web object. This is either a slice or a hotspot that has one or more behaviors attached to it

- Images. These are the images that are displayed in the rollover. In a simple rollover, the first image resides below the trigger object and the second image resides in the target area

In a simple rollover, an image from frame 1 is replaced by one from frame 2. However, for more complex rollovers, the replacement image can be taken from any other frame.

- Frames. Images in a rollover are placed on separate frames within the document

Rollovers can be created using either the Behaviors panel or drag-and-drop techniques. The most basic rollover is known as a simple rollover. This is when an image is replaced by one directly below it when the cursor moves over it. However, it is also possible to create more complex rollovers using the same techniques.

Creating simple rollovers with behaviors

Slices can be inserted over an image by using the Slice tool on the Tools panel and clicking and dragging over the image. Alternatively, select the image and select Edit>Insert> Slice from the Menu bar.

1 Select an image and insert a slice over it. The slice is the trigger object

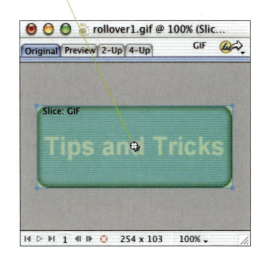

2 Select Window>Frames to display the Frames panel

The menu for the Frames panel can be accessed by clicking the black triangle at the top right of the panel. This provides options for adding frames, duplicating frames and deleting frames.

3 In the Frames panel, click here to add a new or duplicate frame

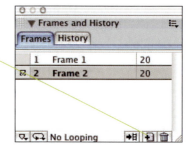

4 Draw a new graphic in the work area or import an image

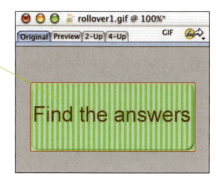

As long as the view button on the Tools panel is selected to show slices/hotspots, then you can select the slice or hotspot in any frame of the rollover.

5 Select either frame in the Frames panel and select the slice or hotspot

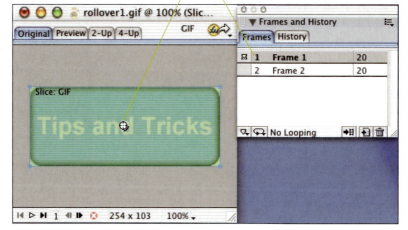

6 Select Window>Behaviors from the Menu bar

Behaviors are Javascript commands that add the interactive element to items such as rollovers.

7 Click here to access the available behaviors

When a behavior is selected, the default event is also selected. An event is an action that triggers the behavior and is usually connected to the actions of the mouse i.e. onClick or onRelease. For a simple rollover the default event is onMouseOver, which means the rollover is activated when the mouse rolls over the image.

8 Select Simple Rollover as the behavior

9 Select the Preview tab and roll over the image with the cursor to see the rollover take effect:

Before the cursor rolls over

After the cursor rolls over

Drag-and-drop rollovers

Creating rollovers with drag-and-drop techniques achieves the same results as using the Behaviors panel, but it can provide more flexibility, particularly when working with more complex rollovers. To use drag-and-drop to create a simple rollover:

1 Select an image and insert a slice over it

The two images or graphics used for a simple rollover do not have to be the same size or shape, but they generally are for elements such as navigation buttons.

2 Select Window>Frames to display the Frames panel

3 In the Frames panel, click here to add a new or duplicate frame

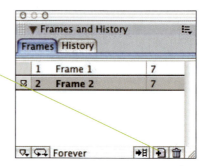

4 Draw a new graphic in the work area or import an image

The slice resides above the images in both frames and so can be selected from either one.

5 Select either frame in the Frames panel and select the slice or hotspot

6 Click here and drag to the top left-hand corner. A blue line loops between the two points

The Swap Image dialog box has a More Options button that can be used to preview the image that will serve as the swap image and also to specify an image from another frame or select an image from a separate file instead.

Rollovers can also be previewed in a browser by pressing the F12 key.

7 The Swap Image dialog box is activated automatically. Select Frame 2 as the location for the second image

8 Click OK

9 Select the Preview tab to see the rollover effect

Creating disjoint rollovers

Disjoint rollovers are ones where the rollover effect i.e. the second image, appears in a different location to the initial image. This is created by placing the disjoint image under a different slice, unlike a simple rollover, where both images are under the same, single slice. Disjoint rollovers can give a very sophisticated appearance to a Web page and they are particularly effective for displaying text in a different location to a trigger object. To create a disjoint rollover:

A disjoint rollover can consist of any combination of images and text, it does not have to be one or the other.

When creating a disjoint rollover, do not make the distance between the two elements too large. If it is, this could create too much unused space when the rollover is displayed on a Web page.

1 Select an image and insert a slice over it. The slice is the trigger object

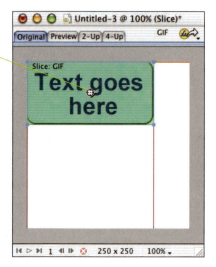

2 Select Window>Frames to display the Frames panel

With a disjoint rollover, the image that is initially displayed remains in place when the cursor is rolled over the trigger object. This displays the second image and so the two images are visible together.

3 In the Frames panel, click here to add a new or duplicate frame

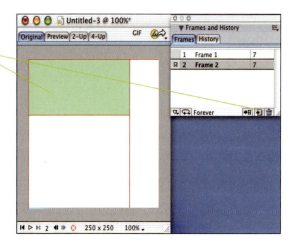

4 Draw a new graphic, import an image, or add text to the work area. Insert it at a different point to the image in frame 1

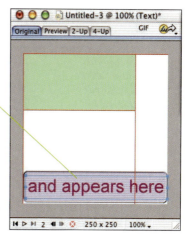

If the slice or hotspot is smaller than the item in the frame then not all of that item will appear when the rollover is previewed. Only the area under the slice will be visible.

5 Insert a slice or hotspot over the item in frame 2

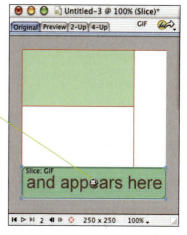

The trigger object for a disjoint rollover can only be linked with one other slice, even though it is possible to put numerous slices on a single frame.

6 Select any frame and click and hold on the slice over frame 1

The disjoint rollover effect can also be achieved by selecting the slice in frame 1 and selecting Swap Image in the Behaviors panel. Then select the image to be displayed as the disjoint rollover.

7 A pointing hand should appear. Drag it down to the item in frame 2. This should create a curved blue line between the two items

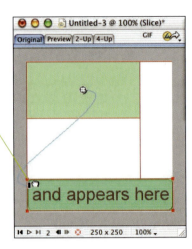

8 The Swap Image dialog box is activated automatically. Select Frame 2 as the item that will appear as the disjoint image. Click OK (as in Steps 7 and 8 on page 123)

Links can be added to a rollover by using the Properties Inspector. For a disjoint rollover, add the link to the trigger object in frame 1.

9 Select the Preview tab or F12 to preview the rollover

When the disjoint rollover has been completed, select Modify> Canvas>Trim Canvas. This ensures that the elements that are exported are no bigger than the largest area of the rollover.

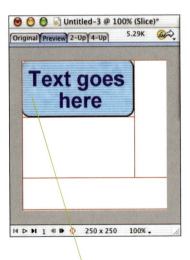

Roll over here and the disjoint effect appears here

Creating pop-up menus

Pop-up menus are created with complex Javascript code and they were once only the domain of programming professionals. However, Fireworks has changed all that and it is now possible for anyone to create pop-up menus, regardless of whether they know the first thing about Javascript or not. This is done through the use of slices and rollovers. Pop-up menus are menus where the user rolls over a graphic and this displays one, or more, subsequent menus. To create a pop-up menu:

Pop-up menus are an excellent navigation device for condensing a lot of items into one area.

1 Create a graphic that will be displayed initially, as part of the pop-up menu

2 Insert a slice over the graphic, either through drawing one with the Slice tool or by selecting the graphic and selecting Edit>Insert>Slice from the Menu bar

3 Select Modify>Pop-up Menu>Add Pop-up Menu from the Menu bar

6 Click here to add the item to the pop-up menu

4 In the Pop-up Menu Editor box, enter a title for the first sub-menu here

If an item on a pop-up menu leads to another level of menus, there is probably no need to include a link with this item. The links should be inserted in the buttons for the final level of the pop-up menu as this is the point where the user will want to access another page.

5 Enter a link here

7 Repeat Steps 4–6 for all of the items to be included in the first level of the pop-up menu:

If pop-up menus have more than three levels it could become confusing for users, since there will be too many sub-menus to navigate through.

8 To create the next level for the pop-up menu, select an item and click here

If you want to move an item in a pop-up menu back to its original level after it has been indented, click on the outdent button (to the left of the indent button).

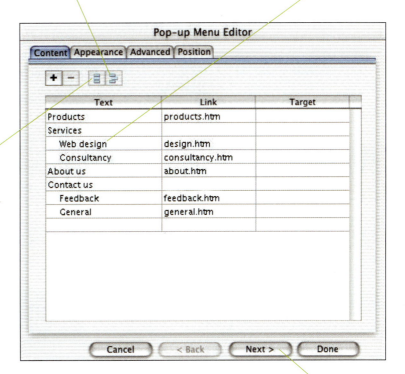

9 Create the structure for the whole of the pop-up menu. Click Next

...cont'd

10 Click here to select
the font and size of
text used on the
pop-up menu

11 Click here to select
the style used for
the pop-up menu

*When
formatting a
pop-up menu,
use a similar
design to the
graphic that was created at
the beginning of the process
(see Step 1).*

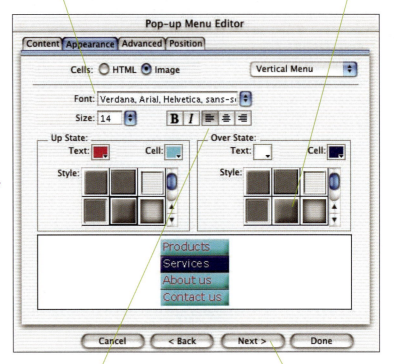

12 Click here to select the
formatting and alignment
used on the pop-up
menu

13 Click Next

The cell padding and cell spacing affects the amount of space between the text and the edge of a button; and between each button. This is the same type of spacing as used in a HTML table.

14 Select the spacing of the text on the pop-up menu

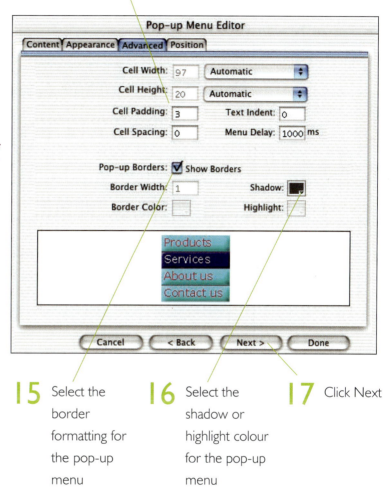

15 Select the border formatting for the pop-up menu

16 Select the shadow or highlight colour for the pop-up menu

17 Click Next

18 Select the position for where the pop-up menu will appear in relation to the main menu item (i.e. the object that will trigger the appearance of the pop-up menu)

For more information about positioning pop-up menus on a Web page see the Fireworks support page on the Web at: www.macromedia.com/ support/fireworks/

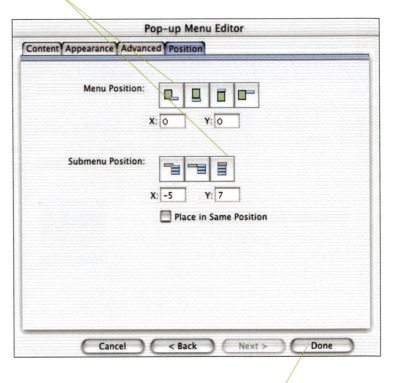

19 Click Done

20 Select the Pointer tool and click and drag to reposition the pop-up menu, if required

Sub-menus on pop-up menus are usually connected to the trigger object i.e. the item that the user rolls over to activate the rest of the pop-up menu.

Once a pop-up menu has been created, it has to be exported before it can be inserted into a Web page. This involves exporting the slices that make up the pop-up menu and also the HTML file which is used to reassemble the pop-up menu in a browser.

21 Preview the pop-up menu. Rolling over one button displays the available sub-menus

Editing pop-up menus

To edit a pop-up menu:

1   Open the pop-up menu file and click on the trigger slice

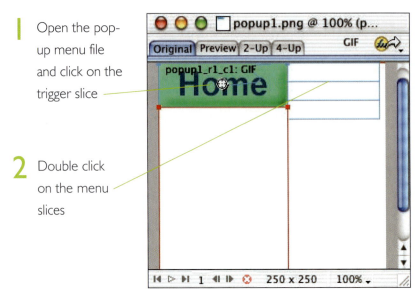

If a pop-up menu is edited, it will have to be exported again so that the newest version is used on any Web pages. Alternatively, if the pop-up menu is being used in Dreamweaver, the Update HTML command can be used in Fireworks to update the menu in Dreamweaver.

2   Double click on the menu slices

3   Apply the editing options in the same way as creating an initial pop-up menu

4   Click Next to access all of the editing options

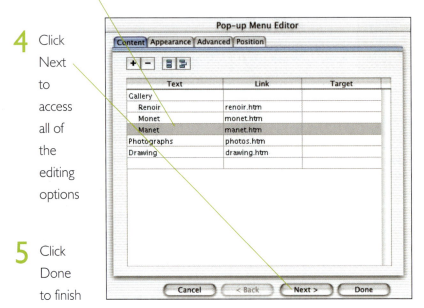

5   Click Done to finish

Combining slices and hotspots

Slices and hotspots can be combined to create another level of sophistication for rollovers. For instance, a slice can be inserted to swap an image or create a disjoint rollover and then a hotspot can be placed on top of it so that only that specific area triggers the rollover. To combine slices and rollovers (this is for a disjoint rollover, but the procedure is the same for a simple rollover too):

Creating a rollover with slices and hotspots gives a greater degree of precision for defining the area which will trigger a rollover. It means that you are not restricted to using complete images as the trigger area.

1 Create an object and add a slice to it

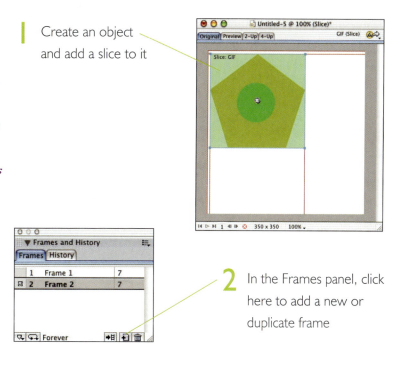

2 In the Frames panel, click here to add a new or duplicate frame

3 Draw a new graphic, import an image, or add text to the work area. Insert it at a different point to the image in frame 1

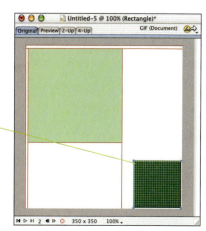

4 Insert a slice over the object in frame 2

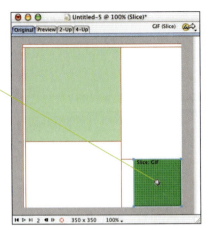

When the hotspot is drawn over the slice, it becomes the trigger object, rather than the slice.

5 Select the slice over the object in frame 1 and select the Hotspot tool from the Tools panel

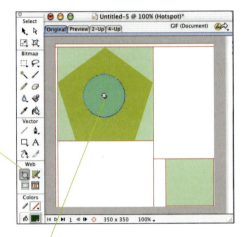

When adding a hotspot that is going to act as the trigger area make sure it is clear to the user that this is where they are meant to move the cursor. For instance, it could be over some explanatory text or a graphic such as an open door. If the user does not know how to activate the rollover, then its effectiveness could be lost.

6 Draw a hotspot on top of the slice

7 Select the Pointer tool and position it over the centre point of the hotspot until it turns into a pointing hand

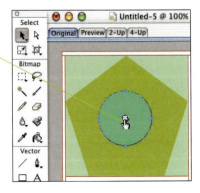

8 Drag from the object in frame 1 to the object in frame 2. This is indicated by a curved blue line

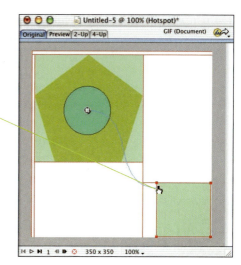

It is possible to add images in numerous different frames and then use these as the swap image, it does not have to be the one in frame 2. It is then possible to change the image if you want the rollover to include a different swap image. This could be useful if you had an e-commerce site displaying different special offers. Each week the rollover could be updated to show a different product by selecting a different frame for the swap image.

9 The Swap Image dialog box is activated automatically. Select Frame 2 and click OK

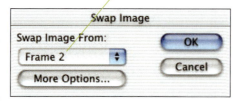

10 When the rollover is previewed or viewed in a browser the disjoint rollover will only be activated when the cursor rolls over the area covered by the hotspot

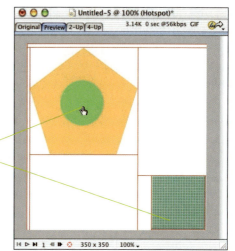

Editing behaviors

The Behaviors panel contains the details of how a rollover is triggered and what happens once this trigger has taken place. These are known as events and actions, respectively. It is possible to edit the events and actions for behaviors and also delete them.

Changing events

The default event for triggering a rollover is onMouseOver i.e. when the mouse rolls over the trigger object the rollover occurs. To change this:

Behaviors can only be added to slices or hotspots, rather than images or graphics created in Fireworks.

1 Click here on the Behaviors panel

Several behaviors can be added to a single slice or hotspot. These are executed in the order in which they appear in the Behaviors panel.

2 Click here to select different events. These are:

- onMouseOut, which is activated when the cursor is rolled over the trigger and then away from it;
- onClick, which is activated by clicking on the trigger;
- onLoad, which is activated as soon as the image is loaded into a browser

onMouseOver
onMouseOut
onClick
onLoad

Adding actions

Actions can be added to a slice or a hotspot through either the Behaviors panel or by clicking on the drag-and-drop handle in the centre of one of these objects:

1 Click here on the Behaviors panel

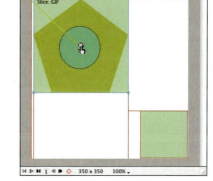

or

Click here on the handle on a slice or hotspot

The Set Text of Status Bar action can be used to display text in the status bar at the bottom of a browser window. When this action is selected, text can be entered into a dialog box and this is what will appear in the status bar. This is a useful device for reinforcing a particular message, but it is best used sparingly on Web pages.

2 Select the required option from the menu that appears after Step 1

Deleting actions

1 Select the action in the Behaviors panel

2 Click here to remove the action

Exporting rollovers

When a pop-up menu is exported, a Javascript file is also exported. The provides the functionality for the menu.

When rollovers have been created they need to be exported so that they can then be included with an HTML Web page. The export process is the same for all types of rollovers and it involves exporting the images that have been created and also the HTML file that contains the necessary code. To export a rollover:

1   Select File>Export from the Menu bar

2   Select a location and enter a name for the rollover

The name of the rollover is used as the root name for all of the images that are created for it.

3   Select HTML and Images

4   Select Export HTML File

5   Select Export Slices

6   Click Save

When a rollover is exported, Fireworks creates a small image file called a spacer (spacer.gif). This is used to ensure that the elements of the rollover are correctly positioned within the HTML table that is created to accommodate them.

7   Check the rollover files are in your file structure

Animation

Animation can add a degree of real style and panache to a website. This chapter shows how to create simple animations in Fireworks and how to apply settings so that they can be exported into other programs.

Covers

Animation in Fireworks | 142

Animation basics | 143

Creating symbols | 144

Animation and the Library | 146

Creating a simple animation | 148

Animation settings | 150

Optimising | 153

Exporting | 154

Editing animations | 156

Onion skinning | 157

Tweening | 158

Chapter Ten

Animation in Fireworks

Although Fireworks does not have the power to create the kind of sophisticated animations that can be produced in a program such as Flash, it can nevertheless be used to create some interesting animated effects. These include banner advertisements, animated logos or small cartoon animations:

 Banner ads were once all the rage on websites but their worth is being questioned more and more these days. However, there is still a place for well-designed and original banner ads.

Banner ads can be created to display different items:

Animated logos can be created for corporate or personal use:

 When creating animated logos, do not loop them continuously i.e. have them playing all of the time. One sequence is usually enough, particularly if people are going to be returning to the page a lot, in which case the animation will be activated again.

Budding cartoonists can give life to their drawings:

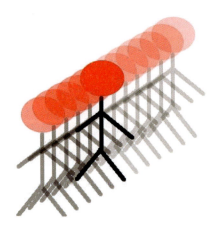

Animation basics

The theory of animation in Fireworks is the same as for creating an animated film: objects are created and then played in a sequence to create the animated effect. This requires working with different elements within Fireworks:

Symbols can be created as buttons, graphics or animations. All of these can then be used within a single Fireworks document.

- Symbols. The objects that are animated are known as symbols. These are normal graphics that are converted into a format that the program can then work with as animation. Symbols can be created from scratch or existing objects can be converted into symbols. When symbols are created they are placed in the Library. Copies of the symbol (known as instances) can then be used in the animation, while the original symbol remains in the Library:

Symbols are placed in the Library and then instances of them can be copied into the work area. Numerous instances can be created from one symbol

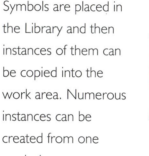

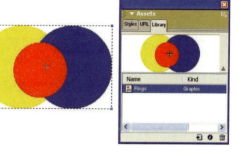

Text blocks can be made into symbols. This is necessary if you want to create animated text.

- Frames. In order for symbols to be animated they have to be placed on separate frames. When the animation is played, the frames are viewed in sequence and this creates the animated effect

Tweening is an animation term that refers to the frames in between two points where an object changes position. Traditionally, in film animation, these are the frames that are created by the less experienced animators.

- Tweening. This is the technique for creating the sense of motion between two points. In one frame the object is positioned at the start point; in another frame it is moved to a different location. Tweening can then be applied to animate it between the two points

Creating symbols

Symbols are the building blocks of an animation. Without them a lot of the functionality of an animation would be lost. Symbols can be created as graphics, buttons or animations. Single graphic symbols can be included in a document and then have animated effects applied to them, while animated symbols can be included as an animation within an animation. Symbols always reside in the Library and they can be created from scratch, or existing documents can be converted into symbols.

If you try and animate an object that is not a symbol, Fireworks will automatically convert it to an animation symbol.

Creating new symbols

1 Open a new document and select Edit>Insert>New Symbol from the Menu bar

When graphic symbols are used to create an animation, the end product is created as a new, animated symbol.

2 In the Symbol Properties dialog box, give the symbol a name and select the type

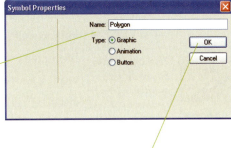

3 Click OK

Graphic symbols are the ones most commonly used in animation. Animation symbols are like small animations that can be used independently or as part of a bigger animation.

4 The symbol window appears over the main document window. Think of this as residing inside the main window

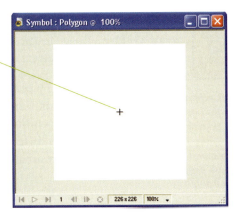

5 Enter the content for the symbol

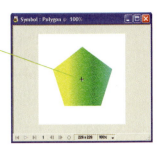

An instance of a symbol is a special type of copy that is referenced to the original symbol rather than just a straightforward copy of it. This means that it does not contain any content in its own right. This can be done because the symbol is created as a vector object rather than a bitmap one, so the instance is just another mathematical equation. This means that numerous instances can be used from the same symbol without increasing the file size of the document. This only changes if the original symbol is edited. When a change is made to a symbol, then this is also applied to all of the instances that have been created from it.

6 Close the symbol window. An instance of the symbol is placed within the work area and the symbol is placed in the Library

Converting objects into symbols

1 Create an object in the work area and select it

2 Select Modify>Symbol>Convert to Symbol from the Menu bar

3 In the Symbol Properties dialog box, give the symbol a name and select the type. Click OK

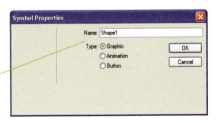

Animation and the Library

Creating instances

All symbols that are created are placed in the Library. They can then be placed within a document as an instance by inserting them into the work area:

Each symbol type is denoted by its own icon.

1 Select a symbol from the list here

2 Drag the symbol into the work area to create an instance

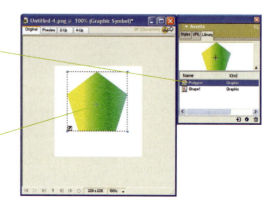

Creating symbols

Symbols can be edited by double-clicking on them in the top panel of the Library. Any changes that are made will affect all instances of that symbol that have been added to a document.

1 Click here to create a new symbol

2 Enter a name and type of symbol. Click OK and follow Steps 3–5 on pages 144–145

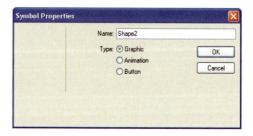

Deleting symbols

If a symbol is deleted from the Library, all instances of it that have been created will also be deleted.

Select a symbol in the lower panel of the Library and click on the wastebasket icon to delete it

Editing the Library

If an instance of a symbol is deleted in the work area, this does not affect the original symbol.

Click here to access the Library menu

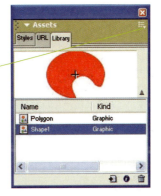

Drag here to expand the Library display area

Creating a simple animation

Simple animations can be created by dragging a symbol from the Library and then animating it, or animating an object that has already been created, in which case it will automatically be converted into a symbol. To create a simple animation:

An instance in the work area is identified by a dotted line around it when it is selected.

Make sure an item is selected before you try and animate it.

The Animate dialog box is looked at in more detail on pages 150–152.

1 Create an instance of a graphic symbol by dragging it into the work area from the Library

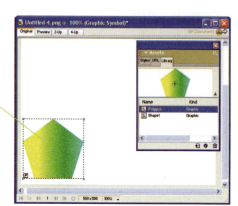

2 Select Modify> Animation>Animate Selection from the Menu bar

3 In the Animate dialog box, leave the default settings as they are. Click OK

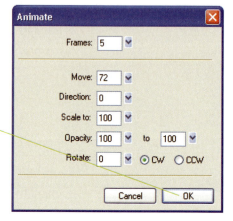

4 This dialog box may appear if the animation requires additional frames. Click OK

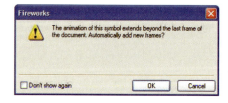

...cont'd

The centre-point of the object in the first frame is green and the one in the last frame is red. The centre-points of the in-between frames are blue. These colours remain the same regardless of the frame currently selected.

5 The centre-point of the instance in the different frames is shown here

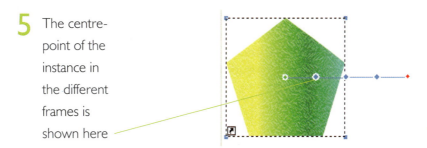

6 In this animation the object will move from left to right

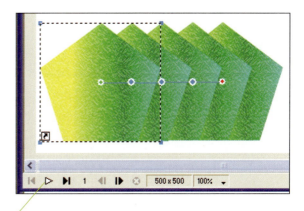

7 Click here to play and stop the animation

8 Select Window>Frames to view the Frames panel

9 Click on a frame to see the position of the object at that point

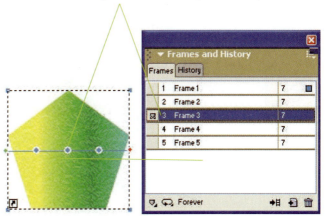

Animation settings

The way that an animation performs can be determined in the animation settings dialog box. This controls the distance an object moves when it is animated, the direction it moves in and its opacity. To determine animation settings:

1 Apply the settings in the Animate dialog box when an animation is first created. Or, select an animation and select Modify>Animation>Settings from the Menu bar

The Animate settings dialog box can also be accessed by right-clicking (Windows) or Ctrl+clicking (Mac) on an animation and selecting Animation>Settings from the contextual menu.

2 Enter a value to specify how far (in pixels) the animated object moves in each frame. Click OK

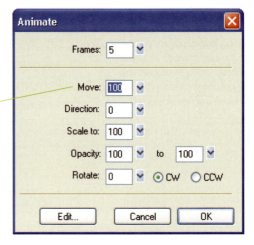

The maximum move value is 250 and the minimum is 0.

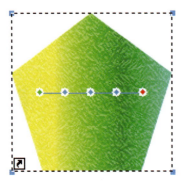

A move value of 100

Select a move value of 0 if you want an object to animate at the same spot e.g. a spinning wheel.

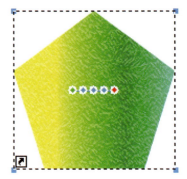

A move value of 20

The direction setting can be changed by either adding a numerical value or by clicking on the down arrow next to the direction box and dragging the dial to the required direction.

3 Enter a value to specify the direction (in degrees) in which the animated object moves. Click OK

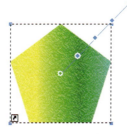

A direction value of 45

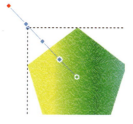

A direction value of 135

If the direction is set to 0, the object will move from left to right in a straight line.

4 Enter a value to specify how the object is scaled i.e. how it changes size when it is animated. Click OK

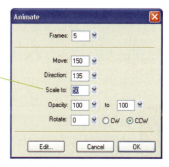

If the scale value is set at 0, this will make the object disappear at the end of the animation i.e. it will start at its normal size and then get progressively smaller until it disappears.

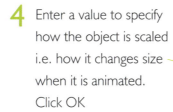

An object scaling to 0

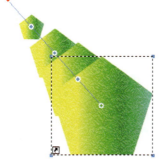

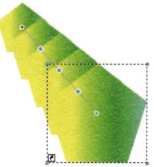

An object scaling to 50

5 Enter a value to specify the opacity i.e. the level of transparency. Click OK

The opacity value in the first box is the one that is applied in frame 1. So if you want an object to begin completely transparent and then fade into view, enter a value of 0 in the first box.

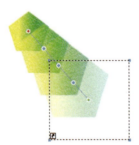

An opacity value of 0 to 100

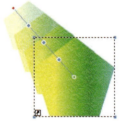

An opacity value of 100 to 0

6 Enter a value to specify the amount (in degrees) that the object rotates during the animation. Click OK

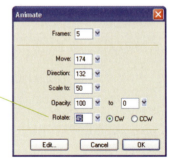

An object can be rotated in a clockwise or a counter-clockwise direction.

A rotation of 45

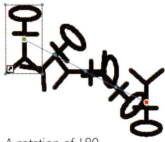

A rotation of 180

Optimising

When an animation has been completed, it has to be optimised and exported so that it is in a suitable format for displaying on the Web. To do this the image has to first be optimised as an animated GIF and then exported. To optimise an animation:

1 Create an animation and select Window>Optimize from the Menu bar:

If an animation is optimised in a format other than an animated GIF, and then exported, the result will be a single frame, static image.

Animated GIFs are created as single files, even though they can contain numerous frames.

2 Click here to select the image format. Select Animated GIF. The settings for an animated GIF are the same as those for a non-animated one

Animated GIFs are larger than comparable static images and so if a lot of them are being used,, downloading time could become an issue.

Exporting

Once animations have been optimised as animated GIFs they can then be exported into a variety of formats, including Flash SWF files.

Setting looping

Before an animation is exported its looping attributes can be set to determine how many times it plays after the initial sequence. To do this:

The looping number applies to the animation after it has played through one time. Therefore, if looping is set to No Looping, the animation will play once and then stop.

Animation that loops Forever, i.e. continuously, can get very annoying after a while and can actually detract from a website rather than add to it.

1 Click here on the Frames panel

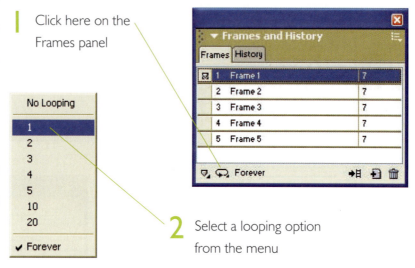

2 Select a looping option from the menu

Exporting an animated GIF

One option for exporting animations is to do so in the same format in which they are optimised i.e. animated GIFs. To do this:

1 Select File>Export from the Menu bar:

2 Give the animation a name and save it as Images Only

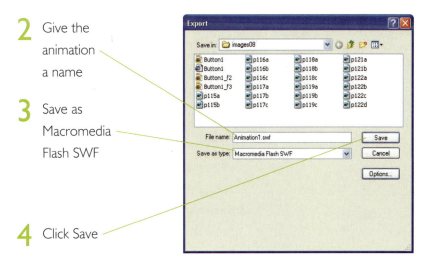

3 Click Save

Flash movies can be incorporated into HTML Web pages. When they are viewed in a browser, the Flash Player has to be installed. This is a plug-in program that enables the browser to play the Flash file. If the Flash Player is not already installed it can be downloaded from www.macromedia.com

Exporting a SWF file

In addition to exporting animations as animated GIFs, they can also be exported as Flash files, which have the SWF file extension. These can then be edited within Flash or inserted directly into a Dreamweaver document. To do this:

1 Select File>Export from the Menu bar

2 Give the animation a name

3 Save as Macromedia Flash SWF

4 Click Save

Editing animations

Modifying paths

When an animation has been created it is then possible to edit the path it takes. This can be done by dragging the animation's path to a new location and all of the frames are updated accordingly. To do this:

1 Create an animation and select it so that its entire path across all frames is showing

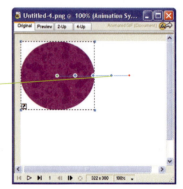

Click on one of the coloured dots on an animation's path to see the attributes of the object in that particular frame.

2 Click and drag here to move the start and end points of the animation. This can also be dragged to change the amount the animation moves between each frame

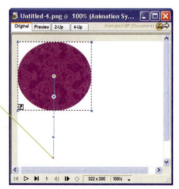

The direction in which an animation moves can also be edited by dragging the start and end points of its path.

3 Click and drag here to move the entire path without changing the amount the animation moves between frames

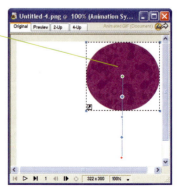

Onion skinning

When working with animations that cover several frames it is useful to be able to see how an object appears in different frames, while still being able to view and edit it in the current frame. This can be done with a technique called onion skinning. This enables you to see an outline of one, or more, other frames, to see the overall progression of the animation. To use onion skinning:

1 Select an animation

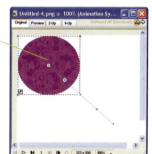

Onion skinning is an animation technique that refers to the practice of placing thin sheets of transparent paper on top of a drawing, to determine the location for the next frame of the animation.

2 Select Window>Frames from the Menu bar

If you have an animation covering a lot of frames, it can be confusing if you set onion skinning to Show All Frames. A better option may be to use Show Next Frame or Before and After. Alternatively, you could create your own settings in the Custom dialog box.

3 Click here to select the onion skinning options

4 Select a frame on the animation's path. Depending on the selection in Step 3, other frames in the animation are visible

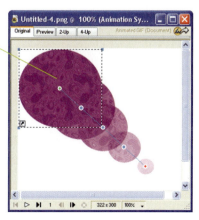

Tweening

Tweening is the process of creating motion between two different points of an animation. If an animation is created as shown on the previous pages, the tweening is inserted automatically. However, it is also possible to create tweening manually, for greater flexibility. To do this:

 The type of tweening that can be done in Fireworks is known as motion tweening.

 In Fireworks you cannot tween instances from two different symbols i.e. a circle and a square. This is known as shape tweening (or morphing) and a program such as Flash is required to achieve this.

1 Create a graphic symbol and insert two instances of it into the work area. Select both of them

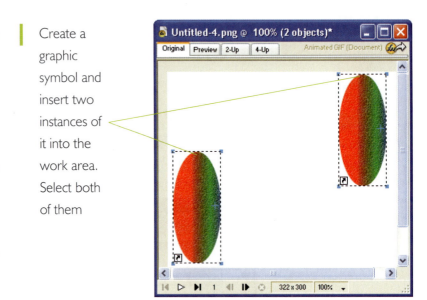

2 Select Modify>Symbol>Tween Instances from the Menu bar

 The Distribute to Frames box can be checked at Step 3, in which case the required number of frames are inserted to accommodate the tween. However, this can be done at a later stage and if it is unchecked it enables you to see the full path of the tween more clearly.

3 In the Tween Instances dialog box, leave the number of steps as the default chosen by Fireworks

and leave the Distribute to Frames box unchecked. Click OK

4 To create a multi-directional tween, insert another instance of the same symbol and position it so that the current tween has to change direction to reach it

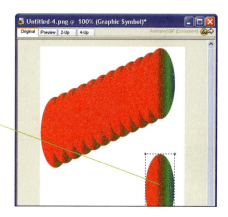

To select two instances at once, click on the first one and then Shift+click on the second one.

5 Select the instance at the end of the first tween and also select the new instance. Repeat Steps 2–3 on the previous page

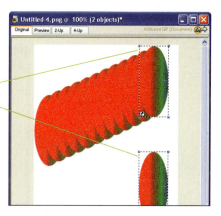

All of the instances can also be selected together by selecting the Pointer tool and dragging an invisible rectangle around all of them in the work area.

6 Choose Select>Select All from the Menu bar

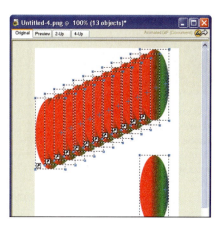

7 Click here on the Frames panel to distribute each instance to a separate frame. This creates the animation when the frames are viewed in sequence

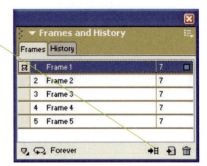

If the instances are not distributed to frames, then the animation will not work.

8 The animation moves in two directions, rather than just in a straight line:

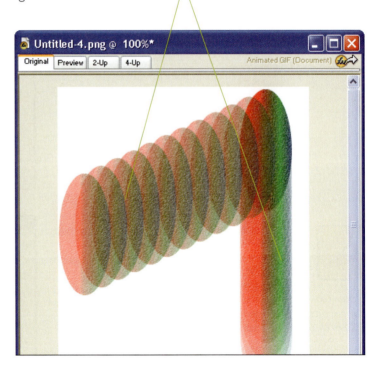

When the canvas of an animation is trimmed, it is done so to the largest area occupied by the complete animated sequence. It does not trim the canvas just to the size of an instance in a particular frame.

9 Select Modify>Canvas>Trim Canvas to make the canvas the same size as the animation i.e. so there is no wasted space

Extending Fireworks

Extensions give Fireworks additional power and versatility. They can be used to create a variety of effects and perform automated tasks. This chapter explains what extensions are, shows how to apply them and also how to obtain new ones.

Covers

About extensions | 162

Applying extensions | 163

Managing extensions | 166

Obtaining extensions | 167

Installing extensions | 170

Using scripts | 171

Chapter Eleven

About extensions

Extensions in Fireworks are small programs that have been developed to give additional functionality. Most of them are created by third-party developers who make them available via the Macromedia website. They are then rated and made available for downloading. Each extension has a link to the developer's own website. Most extensions are free, but some developers charge for the ones on their own sites. Generally, extensions are used to add special effects to images.

To use extensions, the Macromedia Extension Manager must be in place, but this is provided with Fireworks MX. Some extensions are already included within Fireworks MX, while others can be downloaded from the Macromedia Exchange. Alternatively, if you are proficient in Javascript programming, you will be able to create your own extensions.

Another way of extending Fireworks MX is to create scripts that can be applied to different images. This is done by creating a batch process and then saving it as a script. This can then be accessed and applied to other images (see pages 171-172).

To access extensions in Fireworks MX:

The Data Driven Graphics Wizard on the Commands menu is for adding functionality to Fireworks documents, using the XML programming language. This is something that requires a good knowledge of XML before it can be used.

1 Select the Commands menu

2 Select Creative to access the creative extensions

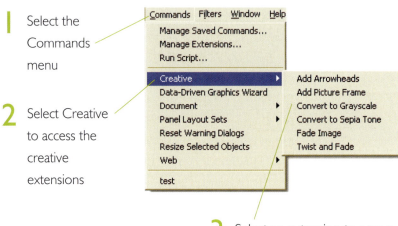

3 Select an extension to access the appropriate dialog box

Applying extensions

Extensions can be applied to vector and bitmap objects. However, some extensions are specific to one type of object or another. To apply extensions to a vector object:

Adding extensions to vectors

1 Select a vector object

BEWARE

If an extension is selected that can only be used on a vector object, it will not operate on a bitmap, and vice versa.

2 Select an extension (see previous page). In this example it is Add Arrowheads

3 Enter the properties in the extension's dialog box

4 Click OK

5 The effect is added to the object

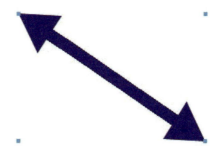

Adding extensions to bitmaps

Select a bitmap image

Experiment with different extensions so that you know what they all do. This will enable you to match extensions to particular tasks, rather than using them just for the sake of it.

2 Select an extension. In this example it is Twist and Fade

...cont'd

3 Enter the properties in the extension's dialog box

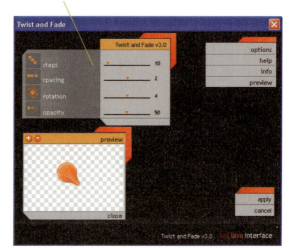

4 Click Apply
(or OK)

5 The effect is added to the image

Use extensions sparingly on images that are going to be used on Web pages, otherwise the effects may become too overpowering.

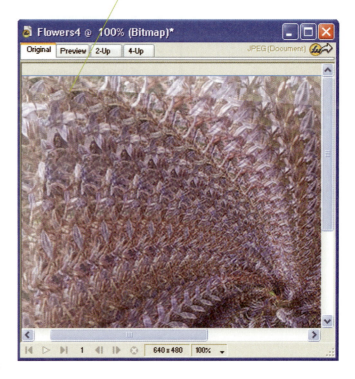

Managing extensions

Extensions can be organised and managed using the Extension Manager that comes preinstalled with Fireworks MX. To use the Extension Manager:

1 Select Commands> Manage Extensions from the Menu bar

Any new extensions that are downloaded and installed will appear in the Extension Manager.

3 Click here to delete a selected extension

2 Click on an extension to select it

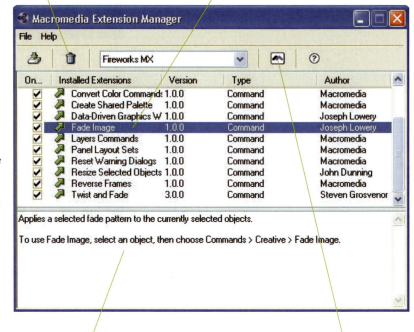

Delete from the Extensions Manager any extensions that you do not use. This will prevent it from becoming too overcrowded.

4 View a description of a selected extension here

5 Click here to connect to the online Macromedia Exchange, where more extensions can be downloaded

Obtaining extensions

Additional extensions can be downloaded from the Macromedia Exchange at www.macromedia.com/exchange

To download additional extensions:

1 Access the Macromedia Exchange and click on the Dreamweaver link. (This also contains the Fireworks extensions)

To use the Macromedia Exchange (and also the online forums) you have to first register with Macromedia. This only requires you to give your email address and select a password. Once you have registered you will have access to all of the online support and development areas and you will also be emailed Macromedia's The Edge online newsletter, containing details of new releases and upgrades.

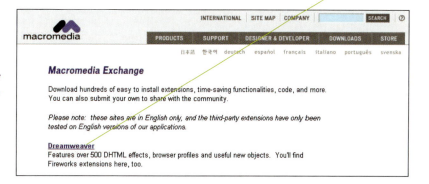

2 Enter you login details and click Login

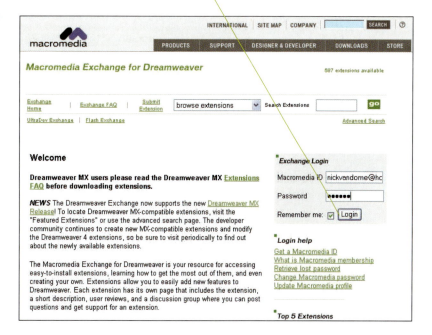

3 In the Search Extensions box, select Fireworks

browse extensions	▼
browse extensions
All Categories
Accessibility
App Servers
Browsers
DHTML/Layers
Extension Development
Fireworks

4 View the details of the extensions here

The Macromedia Exchange is also a very useful resource for extensions for Dreamweaver that can add additional functionality to Web pages.

Macromedia Exchange for Dreamweaver   587 extensions available

Exchange Home | Exchange FAQ | Submit Extension   [browse extensions ▼]   Search Extensions   [   ]   go

UltraDev Exchange | Flash Exchange   Advanced Search

Fireworks extensions   27 extension(s)
(Click on the column name to sort)   Now viewing: **1-20** | 21-27

Name	Author	Date	Version	Rating	Approval	Downloads
3D Objects	Matthew S. Brown	Jun 26, 2002	1.2	4/5	Basic	2379
Animation Text Along a Path	Mengjue	Jul 24, 2002	1.02	No rating	Basic	475
Bend	Kleanthis Economou	Jun 10, 2002	1.0.2	No rating	Basic	3986
BulletBuilder	Joseph Lowery	Apr 22, 2000	1.0.10	4/5	Basic	43494
Button O-Matic	Brendan Dawes	Apr 13, 2000	1.2.0	2/5	Basic	54696
Center in Document Vertically or Horizontally	Nathan Pitman	Feb 12, 2002	1.0.1	3/5	(M)	2836
Change Text Size	John Dunning	Jun 21, 2002	1.0.0	1/5	Basic	687
Color Glow	Edoardo Zubler	Jun 25, 2002	1.0.2	4/5	Basic	4506

5 Click here to access a specific extension

6 Click here to download an extension

Most extensions are very small in size and only take a few seconds to download.

7 Select a location on your hard drive for the extension

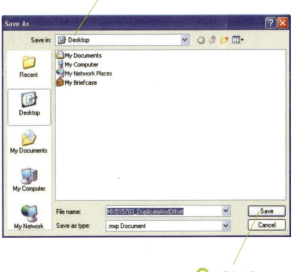

8 Click Save

Installing extensions

Open the Extension Manager and click here

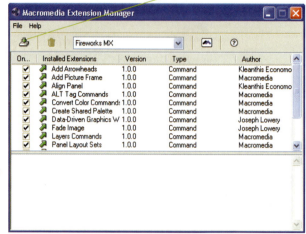

Extensions can also be installed by double-clicking on them in their location on your hard drive.

2 Select the extension to install

Installed extensions appear at the bottom of the Commands menu or, in some instances, at the bottom of the Window menu.

3 Click Install

Using scripts

Scripts are used for functions such as batch processing, where one command is applied to several images. These scripts can be saved and then applied to individual images if required. To use scripts on files:

For more details about creating a batch process and saving the script, see Chapter Twelve page 185.

1 Create a batch process and click on the Save Script button and save the script to your hard drive (for details about creating batch processes, see Chapter Twelve)

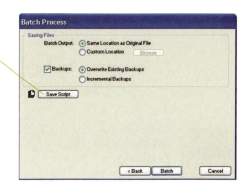

2 Open a file

3 Select Commands> Run Script from the Menu bar

4 Select the required script

5 Click Open

Scripts are an excellent device for applying a single action (or a group of actions) to a large number of files at one time.

6 Select the files to which you want the script to apply

7 Click OK

8 The script is applied to the selected file or files. (In this example the script scales the image so that it is reduced in size)

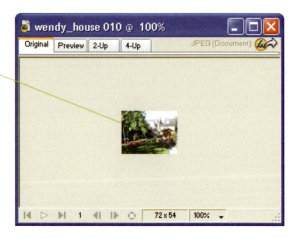

Automating tasks

Fireworks provides the means to perform a variety of tasks across numerous files at the same time. This chapter looks at how editing time can be saved by using automated tasks such as finding and replacing, batch processing and the history panel.

Covers

About automated tasks | 174

Find and Replace | 175

Batch processing | 179

Backing up batch files | 185

History panel | 186

Chapter Twelve

About automated tasks

When working with images you will quickly build up catalogues of various types of images. These could include buttons, rollovers, graphics and animations. During the design process for Web pages or other forms of media, there may be occasions when you want to change an element in a number of files at once. For instance, you may want to change a piece or text, a colour or a URL. This can be done by performing in-built automated tasks. These include:

- Finding and replacing. This can be used to locate a certain item across a group of images and replace it with another item. It can be used with text, fonts, colour and URLs

When you are performing automated tasks, you select the files you want to amend and then apply the task to them. Files can be selected from different directories and they can also be in different formats.

In the Find and Replace panel it is possible to specify elements to be changed

- Batch processing. This can be used to perform certain tasks across a group of images. This includes resizing images, exporting to a different image type and renaming files

The Project Log can be particularly useful if you are working in a team environment.

- History panel commands. The History panel can be used to store groups of commands that are used regularly. When it is required the whole group can be replayed and applied to another item

Another component in the automation process is the Project Log. This identifies files that have been affected by any batch processing and displays a log detailing the changes that have been made. This is a useful way to keep track of files that have been amended.

Find and Replace

The Find and Replace panel is accessed from the Window menu.

Finding and Replacing text

Find and Replace can only be used on PNG files i.e. the proprietary format in Fireworks. This is because images in formats such as GIF and JPEG are viewed as entire graphics, rather than images in their constituent parts. Therefore it would not be possible to identify items such as individual text blocks.

1 Click here and select the criteria for searching for the item

2 Click here and select Find Text

3 Enter the text that is to be found and what is to replace it

4 Click Find

5 All files with the Find text are opened. Select Replace to apply the new text

Finding and Replacing fonts

1 Click here and select the criteria for searching for the item

Any font can be used within images that are going to be published on the Web, rather than just fonts that are available on the user's system. This is because once the image is published the browser views the font as part of the image rather than an individual piece of text.

2 Click here and select Find Font

3 Click here to select a font to change

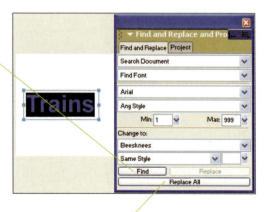

4 Click here to select a replacement font

5 Click Find

Selecting different fonts could have an impact on the overall size of a piece of text, as not all fonts cover the same area, even if they are the same point size. Make sure to check that a change of font has not changed the overall design of an image e.g. gone over the edge of a button or navigation bar.

6 All files with the Find font are opened. Click Replace All (or Replace) to apply the new font

Finding and Replacing colour

I Click here and select the criteria for searching for the item

There is also a Find and Replace option for replacing non-Web-safe colours i.e. colours that are not guaranteed to display in the same way on different browsers over the Web. If this option is selected, non-Web-safe colours are replaced by the nearest Web-safe version.

2 Click here and select Find Color

3 Click here to select a colour to change

4 Click here to select a replacement colour

The Find and Replace colour changes can be applied to strokes and fills together, all properties, or fills, strokes and effects individually.

5 Click Find

6 All files with the Find colour are opened. Click Replace All (or Replace) to apply the new colour

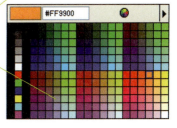

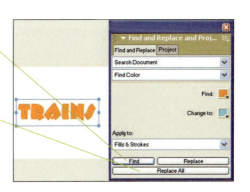

Finding and Replacing URLs

1 Click here and select the criteria for searching for the item

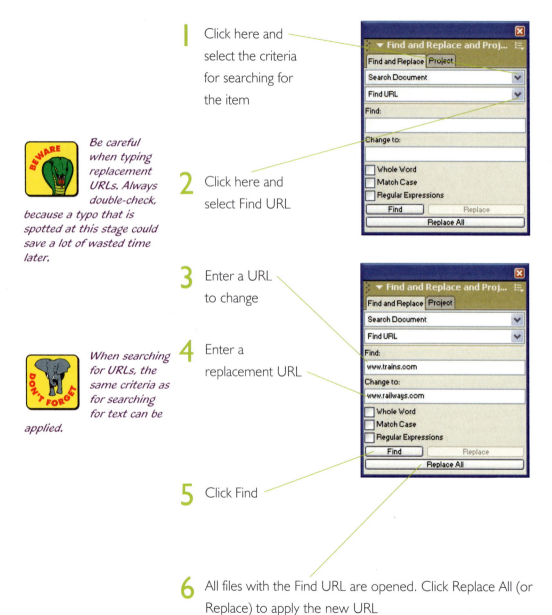

Be careful when typing replacement URLs. Always double-check, because a typo that is spotted at this stage could save a lot of wasted time later.

2 Click here and select Find URL

3 Enter a URL to change

When searching for URLs, the same criteria as for searching for text can be applied.

4 Enter a replacement URL

5 Click Find

6 All files with the Find URL are opened. Click Replace All (or Replace) to apply the new URL

Batch processing

Batch processing can be used to edit various attributes of a large number of files in one operation. To begin batch processing the required files have to be selected:

Batch processing functions can be applied to all types of files, not just PNG ones. The exception to this is the Find and Replace batch function.

1 Select File>Batch Process from the Menu bar

Files for batch processing can be selected from different folders. To do this, add files from one folder, then navigate to a different folder and add files from this one.

2 Navigate to the folder that contains the files to be edited. Select files and click Add to include them in the batch process or click Add All to include all of the files in the folder

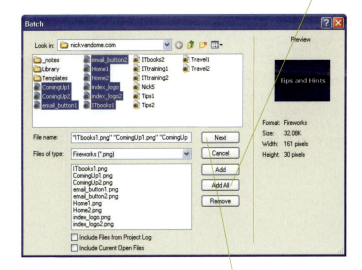

3 Click Next to access the Batch dialog box

Exporting

If you want to convert a batch of files from one format to another, this can be done with the Export function:

1 Select Export and click Add to add this to the commands for the batch process

One reason for exporting a batch of files in one format is if you want to use images in hard copy publications rather than on the Web, or vice versa. For instance, you may want to convert GIFs into TIFFs so they can be printed in a hard copy newsletter or similar publication.

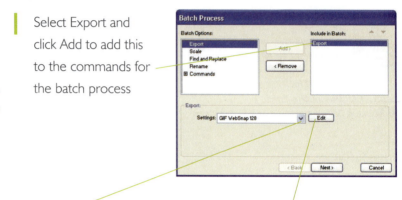

2 Click here to select a file format to which the batch images will be exported

3 Select Edit if you want to export the batch of files to a format other than GIF or JPEG. Select a format in the Export Preview dialog box. Click OK

Several batch processes can be grouped together at the same time. For instance, a batch of files could be exported to a different format and scaled to a different size, in one operation.

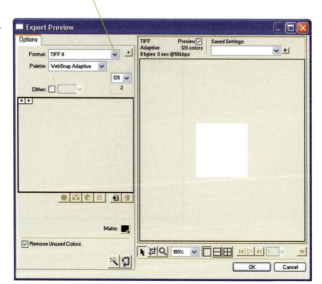

4 The file format is shown here as Custom if a format other than GIF or JPEG has been selected. Click Next

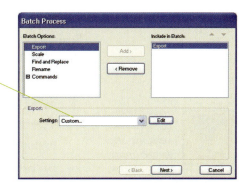

The dialog box that appears at Step 5 can be used to create backup files of the ones that have been changed. For more information about this, see page 185.

5 Click Batch to start the batch process

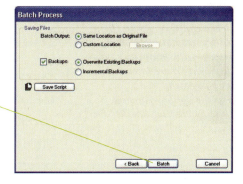

Use the Back button in the Batch dialog box to move back to the previous step of the operation. This can be done at any point before the batch process is started.

6 The batch process will proceed automatically and when it is finished the Batch Progress dialog box will appear. Click OK

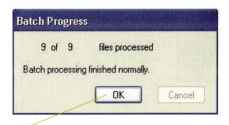

7 Check in the file structure to make sure the required files have been amended

Scaling

Scaling can be used to change the size of a batch of images, for a variety of reasons such as creating thumbnails of images.

Thumbnails are miniaturised versions of a larger image. They can be used as a link to the larger image, so that the user can click on them if they want to see more, or ignore them if they are not interested. This has the advantage of displaying more information on a page and also decreasing downloading time by creating smaller file sizes.

1 Select Scale and select Add to add this to the commands for the batch process

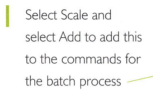

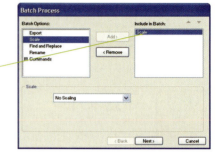

2 Select how the images are to be scaled. This can either be a specific size (in pixels) or a percentage. Click Next

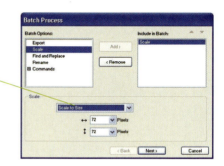

When scaling images that contain text, this can become distorted and appear out of proportion with the rest of the image.

3 Click Batch to start the batch process

4 The batch process will proceed automatically and when it is finished the Batch Progress dialog box will appear. Click OK

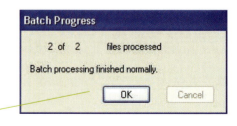

Find and Replace

This can be used to change the same element that appears in numerous files:

1 Select Find and Replace and select Add to add this to the commands for the batch process. Click Next

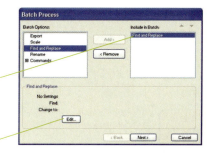

2 Select Edit to choose the required Find and Replace function. These are the same for the Find and Replace functions on pages 175–178. Click OK

3 Select Batch to start the batch process

4 The batch process will proceed automatically and when it is finished the Batch Progress dialog box will appear. Click OK

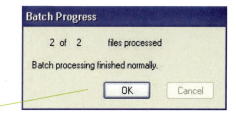

Renaming

This can be used to rename a batch of files by prefixing or suffixing the original name:

1 Select Rename and select Add to add this to the commands for the batch process. Click Next

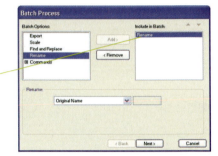

Renaming is a useful option to use in conjunction with exporting files into a different format. If they are renamed at the same time they will be more easily distinguishable from the originals.

2 Select whether to rename the files with a prefix or a suffix. Enter the text in the adjacent box. Click Next

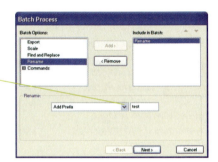

3 Select Batch to start the batch process

4 The batch process will proceed automatically and when it is finished the Batch Progress dialog box will appear. Click OK

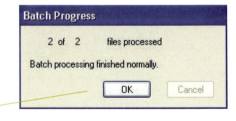

Backing up batch files

When performing batch processes it is important to keep a copy of the files in their original formats, particularly if you are exporting files into a different format. There are various backup settings that can be applied before the batch process is completed. These are selected in the Batch dialog box, before the Batch button is selected:

Scripts can be saved if the batch process contains several actions which you are going to use repeatedly. The script is saved as a JSF file in the same location as the files that are being batch processed. The script can then be opened by selecting File>Run Script from the Menu bar and applied to selected files.

Even if no backup options are selected, the original files of a batch process are still saved in the Original Files folder.

1 Check this box to enable backups to be made

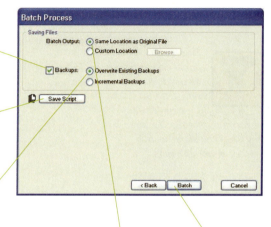

2 Click here to save the script for the current batch process

3 Click here to specify whether backed up files overwrite previous ones or new files are created

4 Click here to specify where the backed up files are stored

5 Click Batch

6 By default, a new folder is created, called Original Files, which stores the original files once they have been batch processed

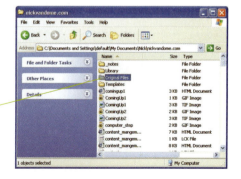

History panel

The History panel keeps track of all of the operations that have been performed on a file. It can be used to save a particular set of actions as a script that can then be applied to other files. To do this:

1 Select Window>History from the Menu bar

The History panel can also be used to undo any actions that have been performed on a file. To do this drag the slider in the History panel upwards.

2 Perform a set of actions, which are then displayed in the History panel

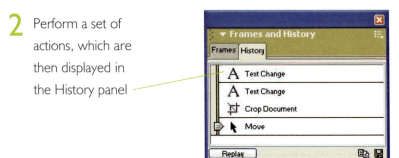

3 Select the actions that you want to save by Shift+clicking on them

4 Click here to save the actions as a command

5 Enter a name for the actions and click OK

6 The script for the actions will now be available at the bottom of the Commands menu, for use on other files

Index

A

Actions
  Set Text of Status Bar   139
Adobe
  Photoshop   8
Alien Skin Splat. *See* Image editing: Alien Skin Splat
Aligning   57
Alternative (Alt) text   89
Animated logos. *See* Animation: Animated logos
Animation
  About   142
  Animate dialog box   148
  Animated GIFs   153
  Animated logos   142
  Animating text   143
  Banner ads   142
  Creating   148
  Distributing to frames   160
  Editing
    Modifying paths   156
  Exporting   154
    Animated GIFs   154
    As SWF files   155
    Looping   154
  Flash   142
  Frames   143
    Centre-point   149
  Instances   145
  Onion skinning   157
  Optimizing   153
  Settings   150
  Symbols   143
    Converting objects into   145
    Creating   144, 146
    Editing   145
  Tweening   143, 158
    Motion tweening   158
    Tween Instances dialog box   158

Arranging   57
  Arrange options
    On Modify toolbar   57
Automated tasks
  About   174
  Batch processing   179
    Backing up batch files   185
    Exporting   180
    Find and Replace   183
    Original Files folder   185
    Renaming   184
    Scaling   182
    Scripts   185
  Find and Replace
    Color   177
    Fonts   176
    Text   175
    URLs   178
  Project Log   174

B

Banner ads. *See* Animation: Banner ads
Behaviors   121
  Actions   121
  Editing   138
    Adding actions   139
    Changing events   138
    Deleting actions   139
  Events   121, 138
Behaviors panel. *See* Panels: Behaviors panel
Bitmaps
  About   26
  Disadvantages   26
  Overall size   26
Blending   102
Blur tool. *See* Tools panel: Blur tool
Button Editor   106, 107
Buttons
  About   106
  Creating   107

Active Area   109
   Copy Up Graphic   108
   Up and Over states   108
Editing   113
   Button Editor   113
Exporting   114
Inserting into Dreamweaver   114
Previewing   114

C

Canvas   18
   Editing size   19
   Rotating   52
   Trim Canvas   31
Cloning   62
Color Mixer panel.   *See* Panels: Color Mixer panel
Creating Web pages   83
Crop tool.   *See* Tools panel: Crop tool
Cropping   61
   Effect on file size   61

D

Default colours
   For strokes and fills   36
Desktop publishing
   File format   72
Distorting   56
Drawing modifiers   36
Drawing tools.   *See also* Tools panel
   Brush tool   39
   Ellipse tool   37
   Line tool   39
   Paint Bucket tool   39
   Pen tool   38
   Pencil tool   39
   Polygon tool   37
   Rectangle tool   37
   Rounded Rectangle tool   37
Dreamweaver.   *See* Macromedia: Dreamweaver

E

Effects
   Adding   45
Erasing   63
Export Preview   23, 70
Export Wizard   71
Exporting.   *See also* Files: Exporting
   Buttons   114
   Hotspots   96
   Rollovers   140
Extensions
   Applying   163
   Explained   162
   Installing   170
   Managing   166
   Obtaining   167
Eye Candy.   *See* Image editing: Eye Candy

F

File formats supported   20
Files
   Creating   18
      Document size   18
   Exporting   23
   Importing   20
   Opening   19
   Save a Copy   22
   Save As   22
   Saving   22
Fills
   Adding   42
Find and Replace panel.   *See* Panels: Find and Replace
   panel
Fireworks.   *See* Macromedia: Fireworks
Fireworks environment   11
Fireworks Forums   24
Fireworks HTML
   Inserting   114

Fireworks Support Center   24
Flash Player   155
Frames panel. *See* Panels: Frames panel
Freeform tool. *See* Tools panel: Freeform tool

GIF   18, 66
Graphical Interchange Format. *See* GIF
Grid   40
    Snap to Grid   40

Help
    Fireworks Help   24
Hexadecimal colours   48
History panel   186. *See also* Panels: History panel
Hotspots   8
    Creating   95
    Exporting   96
HTML   8. *See also* Fireworks HTML
Hyperlinks   8
HyperText Markup Language. *See* HTML

Image editing   32, 33
    Adjusting colour   32
    Alien Skin Splat   34
    Auto Levels   32
    Blurring and Sharpening   33
    Eye Candy   34
    Filters   32
Image maps   95
Images
    Previewing   67

Resizing
    Constrain proportions   81
    From Dreamweaver   81
Importing. *See also* Files: Importing
    From scanners and cameras   21
Info panel. *See* Panels: Info panel
Instances   106. *See also* Animation: Instances
    Identifying   148

Javascript   8, 106, 127
Joint Photographic Experts Group. *See* JPEG
JPEG   18, 66

Lasso tool. *See* Tools panel: Lasso tool
Layers   21
    Adding   99
    Blending   102
    Creating   97
    Deleting   100
    Hiding   100
    Locking   101
    Naming   99
    Selecting   100
    Setting transparency   101
    Stacking order   99
    Web layer   98
Layers panel. *See* Panels: Layers panel
Library   143
    Creating instances   146
    Creating symbols   146
    Editing   147
    Symbols
        Deleting   147
    With animation   146
    With buttons   111
Library panel. *See* Panels: Library panel

M

Macromedia   8
  Dreamweaver   8
  Fireworks
    Adding a desktop shortcut   10
    Cost   9
    Described   8
    Downloading   9
    Installing   10
    Obtaining   9
    System requirements   10
    Trial   9
  Fireworks and Dreamweaver   78
Macromedia Exchange   167–168
  Registering   167
Magnification
  Document window   41
  Menu bar   41
  Zoom tool   41
Making selections   58
  Lasso tool   59
  Magic Wand tool   60
  Marquee tool   58
  Oval Marquee tool   58
  Polygon Lasso tool   59
Marquee tool. *See* Tools panel: Marquee tool
Masks
  Creating   103
  Editing   104
  Marquee tools   103
Menu bar   11, 12

N

Navigation bar
  Editing links   116
  Previewing   116

O

Optimising images
  About   66
  Applying   69
Optimize panel. *See* Panels: Optimize panel
Orientation   52
  Flipping
    Horizontally and vertically   53
  Numeric Transform   53
  Preset Transform   53
  Scale tool   52

P

Paint Bucket tool. *See* Tools panel: Paint Bucket tool
Panels   11, 16
  Answers panel   24
  Behaviors panel   16
  Color Mixer panel   16, 48
  Find and Replace panel   16
  Frames panel   16
  Hiding   15
  History panel   16, 174
  Info panel   16
  Layers panel   16
  Library panel   16
  Optimize panel   16, 68
  Project Log panel   16
  Styles panel   16, 47
  Swatches panel   16
  URL panel   16
  Working with   15
Paths   29
  Composite   29
  Selecting   50
Pen tool. *See* Tools panel: Pen tool
Photoshop. *See* Adobe: Photoshop
PNG   18, 19, 66

Pointer. *See* Tools panel: Pointer tool
Points   29
Pop-up menus   8
  Adding items   128
  As a navigation device   127
  Creating   127, 134
  Editing   134
  Exporting   140
  Levels   128
Portable Network Graphic. *See* PNG
Preview panel   67
Preview tabs   11
Project Log. *See* Automated tasks: Project Log
Project Log panel. *See* Panels: Project Log panel
Properties Inspector   17
Proprietary file format   18

Quick Export   73
  Exporting HTML code   74

Reconstituting tables   92
Rectangle tool. *See* Tools panel: Rectangle tool
Resampling. *See* Resizing: images: Resampling
Reshaping   50
  Freeform tool   50
  Reshape Area tool   51
  Subselection tool   50
Resizing
  Images   31
    Resampling   31
Rollovers   8, 27
  About   118
  Adding links   126
  Creating
    With Behaviors   119
    With drag-and-drop   122

Disjoint   124
Exporting   140
  Spacer image   140
Frames panel   120
Simple   119
Swap Image   123
Trigger object   119
Roundtrip image editing   79

Saving. *See* Files: Saving
Scale tool   52. *See also* Tools panel: Scale tool
Scaling   54
Scripts   171
  Saving   171
  Using as commands   171
Selecting colours   64
Selecting items   28
Skewing   55
Slices   8, 119
  About   86
  Creating   87
    From menu bar   87
    With Slice tools   88
  Optimising   90
  Options   89
  Showing and hiding   89
  Text   91
Slices and hotspots
  Combining   135
Slicing   8
Spacer image. *See* Rollovers: Exporting: Spacer image
Strokes
  Adding   44
Styles panel. *See* Panels: Styles panel
Swatches panel. *See* Panels: Swatches panel
Symbols   106. *See also* Animation: Symbols

T

Text
  Adding   40
  Editing   40
  Formatting   40
  Positioning   40
  Styles   47
Text blocks
  As symbols   143
Toolbars   11
  Main   12
    Functions   12
  Modify   12
Tools panel   11, 13
  Accessing options   13
  Additional options   14
  Blur tool   14
  Crop tool   14, 61
  Default options   13
  Distort tool   56
  Eraser tool   63
  Eyedropper tool   64
  Freeform tool   14, 50
  Lasso tool   14
  Magic Wand tool   60
  Marquee tool   14, 58
  Paint Bucket tool   14
  Pen tool   14
  Pointer tool   14
  Polygon Lasso tool   59
  Polygon Slice tool   88
  Rectangle tool   14
  Reshape area tool   51
  Rubber Stamp tool   62
  Scale tool   14, 52, 54
  Skew tool   55
  Slice tool   88
  Subselection tool   50
Transparency   75. *See also* Layers: Setting
    transparency
  Index transparency   75
Trim Canvas. *See* Canvas: Trim Canvas
Tweening. *See* Animation: Tweening

U

Undo function   12

V

Vector selections   28
Vectors   27
  About   27
  Advantages   27
  Identifying selections   28
  Moving   30
  Reshaping   30

W

Web authoring   78
Web design   8
Web layer. *See* Layers: Web layer
Web-safe colours   48
Work area   11